THE King's DAUGHTER

THE King's DAUGHTER

"…MINE EYES HAVE SEEN THE KING…" ISAIAH 6:5

RAJKUMARI MOKSHA

THE TRUE STORY OF A HINDU WOMAN
DISCOVERING HER WORTH IN JESUS CHRIST

THE KING'S DAUGHTER
Copyright © 2023 by Rajkumari Moksha

All scripture quotations are taken from the King James Version, which is in the public domain.

The content of this publication is based on actual events. Names have been changed to protect individual privacy.

Softcover ISBN: 978-1-4866-2336-5
Hardcover ISBN: 978-1-4866-2337-2
eBook ISBN: 978-1-4866-2338-9

Word Alive Press
119 De Baets Street Winnipeg, MB R2J 3R9
www.wordalivepress.ca

WORD ALIVE
—P R E S S—

Cataloguing in Publication information can be obtained from Library and Archives Canada.

Now unto the *King* eternal, immortal, invisible, the only wise God, be honour and glory for ever and ever. Amen. (1 Timothy 1:17, emphasis added)

Kings' daughters were among thy honourable women… Hearken, O daughter, and consider, and incline thine ear; forget also thine own people, and thy father's house; So shall the king greatly desire thy beauty: for he is thy Lord; and worship thou him… *The king's daughter* is all glorious within… (Psalm 45:9–11, 13, emphasis added)

Thine eyes shall see the *king* in his beauty… (Isaiah 33:17, emphasis added)

And they *shall be mine*, saith the LORD of hosts, in that day when I make up *my jewels*… (Malachi 3:17, emphasis added)

DEDICATION

For the LORD is a great God, and a great
King above all gods. (Psalm 95:3)

...our Lord Jesus Christ...
who is the blessed and only Potentate,
the King of kings, and Lord of lords...
(1 Timothy 6:14–15)

I humbly dedicate this book to the Lord Jesus Christ, for the
majesty of His grace and mercy, and for the awesome divine
love He freely, abundantly, and eternally made available to me!

...heaven opened, and behold a white horse; and he that
sat upon him was called Faithful and True...

And he was clothed with a vesture dipped in blood: and
his name is called The Word of God...

And he hath on his vesture and on his thigh a name written,
KING OF KINGS, AND LORD OF LORDS. (Revelation
19:11, 13, 16)

PREFACE

*For thus saith the high and lofty One that
inhabiteth eternity, whose name is Holy;
I dwell in the high and holy place, with
him also that is of a contrite and humble
spirit, to revive the spirit of the humble,
and to revive the heart of the contrite ones.*
(Isaiah 57:15, emphasis added)

Throughout my forty-six-year journey as a Christian, several people, including both believers and unbelievers in the Lord Jesus Christ, have encouraged me to pen my story, which I started doing in 1977.

Initially, I typed with two fingers on loose-leaf lined paper, inserted into an old manual aqua-coloured Brother typewriter that housed a worn double-coloured ink ribbon. My writing has been ongoing with continual direction and approval from the Lord Jesus; however, I have worked toward completion more seriously over the past ten years.

Now, I use an up-to-date word processing program on a desktop computer, progressing to typing with four fingers! Despite several interruptions in this work, the Lord has faithfully used various people to nudge and prod me along the way, always reminding me of the urgency of its prompt completion.

This book has been written prayerfully and truthfully according to the best of my childhood memories, with the help of the Lord Jesus. It was not written to offend anyone, nor to expose mistakes made by various people, nor to make allegations. It is not my intention to degrade or write disparagingly about anyone's character. I attribute any opposition to me as arising from the upbringing of those mentioned, due to their culture and religion and what they believe or believed. For this reason, to protect the identity of these people in the story, all names and locations have been changed.

My Sanskrit pen name "Rajkumari"[1] means a daughter of a king—a princess—and "Moksha"[2] means salvation or freedom from judgment.

This is a book about my journey as a Hindu girl struggling in my early years to find answers and meaning to life's basic vital questions: *Who are we? Why are we here? What is the purpose and meaning of life? Where is there hope in life? How can we find reason for living?*

I trust this book will answer your questions about the meaning of life and the truth about our existence on the earth, as I reveal to you the only Way to find the answers to these complex questions: the Lord Jesus Christ.

Jesus said, *"I am the way, the truth, and the life: no man cometh unto the Father, but by me"* (John 14:6, emphasis added).

Neither is there salvation in any other: for there is none other name under heaven given among men, whereby we must be saved. (Acts 4:12)

---

[1] https://www.yourdictionary.com/rajkumari
[2] https://en.wikipedia.org/wiki/Moksha

Under the grips of Hinduism, my spiritual blindness was vanquished by the light of the gospel of the Lord Jesus Christ.

To open their eyes, and to turn them *from darkness to light, and from the power of Satan unto God,* that they may receive forgiveness of sins… (Acts 26:18, emphasis added)

This book culminates with me finding answers beyond my expectations from a merciful and gracious God I never knew loved me infinitely, unconditionally, and eternally. I am awed by the relationship I now have with Him, surpassing all of my expectations.

I share about an amazing God, whose Son—the Lord Jesus Christ—delights to reach out in our difficult and unique circumstances so He can reveal His everlasting love, abundant grace, enduring mercy, and desire to make us part of His family.

But God commendeth *his love toward us,* in that, while we were yet sinners, Christ died for us. (Romans 5:8, emphasis added)

You will witness a transformative change: a lowly, worthless girl given the privilege of being the daughter of the Almighty God, the King. Although I was undeserving, I became the King's daughter—a truly miraculous occurrence!

I will greatly rejoice in the LORD, my soul shall be joyful in my God; for he hath *clothed me with the garments of salvation,* he hath covered me with the robe of righteousness… as a bride adorneth herself with her jewels. (Isaiah 61:10, emphasis added)

May you see the sufficiency and completeness of Christ's work in my life and be encouraged, inspired, directed, and attracted as you taste for yourself that the Lord is good! *"O taste and see that the Lord is good: blessed is the man that trusteth in him"* (Psalms 34:8).

May you also understand the events of your life through God's perspective, apply His principles to difficult circumstances, and perceive the *glorious* side of every event you go though.

For I know the thoughts that I think toward you, saith the LORD, *thoughts of peace*, and not of evil, to give you *an expected end.* (Jeremiah 29:11, emphasis added)

But as it is written, Eye hath not seen, nor ear heard, neither have entered into the heart of man, the things which *God hath prepared for them that love him.* But God hath revealed them unto us by his Spirit... (1 Corinthians 2:9–10, emphasis added)

CONTENTS

Chapter 1

EARLY YEARS IN KENYA

*…God hath from the beginning chosen
you to salvation through sanctification of
the Spirit and belief of the truth…*
(2 Thessalonians 2:13, emphasis added)

My name is Rajkumari Moksha. I was born in Nairobi, Kenya, East Africa to Hindu parents from India.

In the sixties, the president of Kenya, Jomo Kenyatta, welcomed immigrants from India and was supportive of the Indian community, as they made a positive contribution to his country's economy. Our primary community was made up of these Indian immigrants, who were trying to establish a more prosperous life outside of India. My dad came because he craved a life of better opportunities and education for himself, his wife, and his children, which he had lacked growing up in a small village in Punjab.

After a marriage arranged by both sets of parents, my dad decided to settle in Nairobi with his new bride, as did my maternal grandparents. My firstborn brother, Sohna, four years older than me, being a boy, held a position of favour in the opinion of my parents.

During my early years in Nairobi, my Hindu cultural and religious roots were established by my family. We were sheltered from most exposure to the outside world, although we did listen to the radio and exchange information through conversations within our middle class community.

I had heard about the Beatles, Elvis Presley, and Muhammad Ali—or Cassius Clay, as he was then called. The "cha-cha-cha" was a dance one of my aunts, Alka (someone I considered a "rebel"), tried to demonstrate to us. She was my mother's youngest sister who would experiment with the beehive or French twist hairdos, and wore knee-length "bouffant" style dresses. She baked western-style cakes as best she could in a *githi*, a small coal stove placed on the floor. The cakes had a thick charred crust, but still tasted quite delicious after one scraped off the burnt bottom. Mini hourglass-contoured bottles of Coca-Cola were the common soft drink of the day, as Fanta and orange squash (a concentrated drink diluted with water) were reserved for company.

Outside of this minimal western interference, I was solely exposed to Indian culture: customs, traditions, festivals, and religion. I had Indian friends, ate Indian food, lived in an Indian community, and dressed in more-or-less Indian clothing: cotton frocks hand-made by my mother. In short, I was essentially Indian—Hindu, to be exact!

We lived in a two-storey L-shaped building made up of many apartments or "flats." On the adjoining two sides, there was a low concrete wall at the remaining periphery. The central square courtyard was where all the community functions would be carried out.

We were a close-knit community, everyone knowing each other's business, and no one could hide any personal intimate life details without the rest of the courtyard talking about them. We just seemed to be blissfully content with one another, gossip and all.

For example, everyone knew and whispered about the family living in the so-called servant's quarters apart from the rest of the building, where the drunk husband mistreated his wife. The adults pitied her but never pried with too many questions. Even at the age of five, I knew that there was something odd about that situation.

Then there was the common sight of a disabled adult woman in a reclined wheelchair on the balcony that went along the main floor. Here she had a bird's eye view of all the activities of the courtyard. As she sat like a queen, propped up with pillows and covered with bedding, her head hung over loosely while others fussed over her—especially her mother, who lovingly sopped up her drool. The women in the flats consoled and admired the mother for her persistent care. For me, it was my ambition to stay as far away from this invalid as possible. Not only did she emit a foul odour, but I was afraid of the audible random noises and grunts that escaped from her warped, uneven mouth. Although her distorted, pale face frightened me, I was amused and almost jealous at how well she was cared for.

One day, she was brought down to the sunny courtyard when suddenly a hand snatched me and dragged me over to her, calling out in Punjabi, expecting me to greet *"her"*: "Ajaa!" "Hethe-aja!" I stood frozen and speechless, standing in such proximity to someone I considered so repulsive. At that moment, I agreed with myself that it would be the last time I would ever come near anyone that looked like *"her."*

Also, in one of the flats at the lower far side lived a Caucasian family. It was unthinkable to have much to do with *"them."* I instinctively knew it would not be tolerated if I went wandering in that direction—*Because they are white,* I thought. No one ever talked about *"them"* or to *"them."* They seemed mysterious. I never saw them come out or associate with us, but one day, I curiously wandered over to *that* part of the building. A novel feeling to be in this forbidden domain… when unexpectedly the door opened and the white woman (or *memsaab,* a Hindi term I had heard family use to refer to *"her"*) invited me in. I thought she seemed to be anticipating visitors or watching for them to approach her flat. Wanting to make a good impression, she quickly handed me some marzipan cookies formed in the shape of orange carrots with green tops. Next to my grandmother's, these were the best cookies I had ever tasted. There were bright decorations in her home that were peculiar, but also strangely lovely.

Upon going home, I was immediately scolded and ordered to never enter *"their"* home or talk to *"them"* again. I never found out how my parents knew! Gossipy neighbours, perhaps? I never ventured in that direction again, but always reminisced about the visit and the delightful cookies I was offered.

> According as he [Christ] hath *chosen* us in him before the foundation of the world, that we should be holy and without blame before him in love... (Ephesians 1:4, emphasis added)

> Ye have not chosen me, but I have *chosen* you... that ye should go and bring forth fruit... (John 15:16, emphasis added)

Chapter 2

NAIROBI, "COOL WATER"

Ho, every one that thirsteth,
come ye to the waters, and he that hath
no money; come ye… without money
and without price.
(Isaiah 55:1)

The word Nairobi means "cool water"[3] in Maasai. Despite the proximity of Kenya's capital city to the equator, due to its elevation of over 5,000 feet, the subtropical climate has an average temperature of twenty-four degrees. This city is a refreshing oasis not simply for vegetation, but for life in general.

I would happily play with my friends in the courtyard on countless warm, sunny days. I longed to run and catch gorgeous butterflies with my hands. Coloured powder would stain my fingers as I held one, and then to my dismay I would realize I had injured another wing. Laying it gently down onto the ground, I would watch it stumble, attempting to walk, but failing to do so as it was now imbalanced. As I sadly observed the stunning insect, I understood it would no longer be able to fly and be free because it was so damaged. I would promise myself that I would never hold

---

[3] "Nairobi." *Wikipedia.* http://en.wikipedia.org/wiki/Nairobi (accessed September 25, 2021).

another butterfly… but again at the next opportunity, I wouldn't be able to resist holding an object so strikingly beautiful.

We weren't allowed to leave the property surrounding the building, but at times I would find myself lost in the rows and rows of tall green stalks of corn growing in the farming fields nearby. The sheer delight of being outside in the glowing sunshine, handling the distinct black rich soil, was thrilling. No wonder Nairobi was nicknamed the "Green City in the Sun"!

Sometimes my friends and I would go to the ponds in the adjoining fields after a heavy rainfall, looking for tadpoles. We would hold them in our hands to examine their slimy bodies and varying shapes as they wiggled, quite discontented to be out of water.

Watching the stunning bright green three-inch grasshoppers was intriguing. I could never run fast enough to catch one as they hopped away!

The worst insect in my opinion was the dreaded caterpillar. At certain times of the year, Nairobi would have an epidemic of these caterpillars all over the grass. Everything would be covered with the small creatures. Walking to and from school meant dodging them on the sidewalks.

The concrete building where we lived had multiple deep ridges along the blocks of stone on the outside walls. Six-inch brown lizards would perpetually maneuver into the many crevices and scurry around curiously. They never seemed to get inside the building, nor did they ever seem to land on the ground. I would stare at these quick-moving creatures looking busy, purposeful, and free.

One day, I accompanied Aunt Alka on a rare visit to the home of a sick friend of the family. The ill woman appeared bald and had artificially pencilled-in eyebrows. What interested me most was her little monkey on an incredibly long leash. This cute dark skinny creature would spontaneously climb up onto the roof and move in every direction around the house in very little time. It was frisky and full of energy, constantly scampering around. We were told to mind our belongings as it could instantly grab whatever it wanted! *What independence it has. What a free-spirited creature,* I thought, *even though it is on a leash.*

One day, some neighbours left their talking parrot with us to care for while they were away. Dressed in gorgeous red and blue plumage, sporting a huge turned-down beak, it sat proudly on a post in its large metal cage, which was placed on a table in our tiny front hall. At night, a blanket would be thrown over its cage to keep it quiet and allow it to fall asleep. During the day, its endless chatter amused and entertained me. We were instructed to feed it hot cayenne peppers to supposedly improve its talking ability. It amazingly reproduced the Swahili call of the vendors in the neighbourhood who came around to collect empty glass bottles and boxes: "Chuppa-dubba! Chuppa-dubba!" It also mimicked, with the same tone and urgency, the way my neighbour called out to my mother by name! Even though it was caged, it seemed content, probably not knowing any better. I was sorry to see it leave our home to return to its owner.

These were some of the natural wonders I loved in my hometown. It was my little paradise—Nairobi.

...created all things by Jesus Christ. (Ephesians 3:9)

Jesus... said... If thou knewest the gift of God... thou wouldest have asked of him, and he would have given thee *living water.* (John 4:10, emphasis added)

Chapter 3

COURTYARD EVENTS

For he satisfieth the longing soul, and
filleth the hungry soul with goodness.
(Psalm 107:9)

How could one resist taking advantage of the warm sunshine and long beautiful days outside, with the courtyard bustling and buzzing with activity, noise, people, and life?

Women gathered in the central area to put together lovely flower garlands. I excitedly found a place at the table, threading fragrant orange marigolds or delicately scented white and yellow plumeria. My childish little fingers ran through the fresh, soft, velvety petals—nearly spoiling them. Sometimes while threading the flowers, my needle would pierce the wrong portion of the base and the whole flower would fall apart, ending up in the discard pile. I seemed to contribute more to that pile than to the garlands themselves! Their perfume—their beauty—was used to adorn stone gods and goddesses for religious events, for an approaching wedding, or to honour a special person. Still, the fine magnificence of these blossoms entranced me. I wanted to keep them nearby, sticking my nose into them and sniffing the luxurious fragrance, but instead I watched as they got boxed and taken away.

Special days, weddings, and religious ceremonies always aroused our little community with lively excitement as they brought everyone together to celebrate in the courtyard. People would mill around busily, setting up canopies and equipment. Unnoticed by the busy adults, the children often congregated around a huge, rented chest freezer. It was packed with bottles of Coca-Cola resting comfortably on ice. The bigger and stronger children would pry open the little glass bottles with the attached bottle opener on the side of the freezer for us little ones. We needed to hide them from the adults so we could impishly indulge in one bottle after another. I loved the cold, sweet taste of Coca-Cola, guzzling it down so quickly that the cold bubbles would climb painfully up my nose and settle in my brain! It was one of the few store-bought pleasures we enjoyed as children.

Sometimes, the ladies from the flats would spend a whole day making biscuits to be baked in a rented oven placed in the centre of the courtyard. The fresh sweet aroma arose throughout the entire courtyard to tantalize senses craving for a taste of the golden-brown, melt-in-your-mouth biscuits. My grandmother, Mamaji, had perfected the envied recipe, which she generously shared. Hundreds of cookies would be baked and then passed amongst the people of the courtyard.

Other times, peppery dough for hundreds of *papar* or *papadum* would be rolled into thin rice or lentil flour crepes. These would be sun-dried to bake later, after which they would be served as an appetizer to accompany an Indian meal. It was a community project characterized by the excited chatter of all the women, like birds happily pecking a treasure of worms and seeds, all contributing to the latest gossip. Occasionally, someone would hand me some of the delicious, smooth peppery dough, still raw, as I stood patiently waiting for a taste. As I fought with the sticky mess in my mouth, my glands worked overtime, enjoying the spicy delicacy. Despite the nippy bite on my tongue, I always hoped for more.

There was so much gaiety and commotion during preparation for religious holidays. Some of the other girls my age would be arrayed in intense, multi-coloured, handmade two-piece Punjabi suits, often accompanied with flowing chiffon scarves bordered with gold thread tassels. The pretty little girls dazzled as they sported their little tailored outfits to everyone's admiration. I hoped someone would pay attention to me as I enviously watched these little girls arrayed in so much brilliance. *How can I ask to have such an outfit made for me? Does anyone notice that I do not have one?* I wondered.

So much detailed care was given to make each event enjoyable and vivid. Diwali, or the Indian New Year, was so exciting—perhaps my favourite. The concrete windowsills were adorned with candles. Sweet Indian delicacies, gifts, and money were distributed from flat to flat. Relatives visiting us would hand me cash in British currency.

Sometimes we would go to a community park at night, with many people dressed in intensely-coloured Punjabi suits. We danced interminably around images of Hindu gods posted on a brightly lit large centre column, at the same time noisily striking wooden sticks together to celebrate some mythological victory. The girls and women looked like bright birds fluttering around aimlessly and rhythmically in a circle, creating a monotonous clamour for hours. Once, as a finale, a mythological statue was burned to honour a battle of the gods' victory. I loved the colours, the noise, the crowd, and just being together.

A Hindu festival called Holi was another exciting event. Everyone in the community would go around throwing vibrant dye powder on each other. We wore old clothes, laughed, and tried to avoid being attacked, but ultimately we all got smothered head to toe, walking around like striking creatures from an Amazonian jungle. Understanding neither the importance nor the meaning, I enjoyed the excitement and the fun, but most of all the finished colours that created an impressionist artist's work on our bodies.

Beyond the walled-in area of the courtyard were open fields, where more buildings went up as the demand for housing got greater. Sometimes, construction crews would find poisonous snakes as they dug to pour a foundation. The news would spread throughout our little Hindu community. Everyone would be terrified for a while, but life went on after the news was forgotten and conversation moved to other topics.

Each evening, we participated in activities such as going for walks, gathering for calisthenics, or playing badminton. In those early years, these activities fulfilled my innate desire to belong and enjoy the gaiety of life in this temporary paradise.

This was my home in Nairobi. All the people of the flats were like one big happy family. I felt so secure and safe.

...Jesus said... I am the bread of life: he that cometh to me shall *never hunger*; and he that believeth on me shall *never thirst*. (John 6:35, emphasis added)

Chapter 4

DOG ENCOUNTER

Yea, though I walk through the valley of
the shadow of death, I will fear no evil:
for *thou art with me*; thy rod and
thy staff they comfort me.
(Psalm 23:4, emphasis added)

Before my grandparents moved to our building of flats, they lived in a rented bungalow which backed onto Nairobi National Park. Wild pink rosebushes with sharp thorns adorned the front of the modest one-storey white building. A short wall along the front marked off a small yard. The backyard, which once flourished with numerous fruit trees, was surrounded by a thick ten-foot-high concrete wall with pieces of jagged glass jutting from the top edge. It was here that my grandfather's watchdog was once poisoned by robbers attempting to get into the yard.

At sunset, tall Maasai warriors could be seen running in single file down the path along one side of the house, carrying their pointed spears. Fearful of being noticed as we spied from a bedroom, we would switch to the back window, watching the warriors perform their evening ritual dance in the open fields behind the high walls. Chanting noisily in unison, holding their long spears vertically, we could see their tall, brightly-clad bodies bobbing up and down. The scene terrified me.

The neighbouring house owned a watchdog, which was kept in a gated area to protect their property from the wild animals and robbers. It was purposely underfed to encourage its aggressive nature. I soon experienced the consequences of its vicious temper!

One day, as I stood near an open patio back door, this black medium-sized dog left its yard through a gate which had been accidentally left open, entered my grandfather's house, and came charging, digging its teeth into my back. Somehow, I was rescued. My Aunt Alka brought me into a bedroom to clean the wound with a disinfectant called Dettol as I whimpered in pain.

While I was still trying to forget the first incident, the same dog got loose and bit me a second time on my back. Even though my brother Sohna was present to intervene this time, I still felt I should have been better protected from harm. Once again my aunt tried to console me as she treated my wound, which seemed superficial this time.

I wondered why this dog had hurt me twice, and why little provision had been made to prevent me from harm. I developed a dog phobia. Even seeing a dog from a distance made me sweat profusely—heart pounding, breathing heavily, feeling vulnerable and insecure, in a panic mode, I wanted to run... but not to be chased! The anxiety made me chant the names of Hindu gods, expecting them to protect me.

> *The name of the* LORD *[Jesus] is a strong tower: the righteous runneth into it, and is safe.* (Proverbs 18:10, emphasis added)

Chapter 5

MAMAJI, THE NURSE

...I am the LORD that healeth thee.
(Exodus 15:26)

My grandparents moved from their house to a flat on the second floor at the other end of the building where we lived. It was much bigger than ours.

They had a large kitchen, a washroom and a separate bathing room, a spacious bedroom, and a living room. Two daughters and two sons, all young teens and young adults, lived with them. My mother—the eldest—was their only married child.

Outside the walls of the courtyard was a long strip of land covered by gravel. Since I was not allowed to stroll into the grassy fields nearby, I ran here as fast and as often as I could. It was the usual ritual of falling, picking off the fragments of sharp gravel gouging my knees, and heading over to the flat of my maternal grandmother—Mamaji—for some loving amateur nursing care.

Mamaji would tenderly clean the wounds with Dettol and bandage my knees. Days later, she would coax me to remove the infected bandages, seeping with ooze. After gently wiping off the yellow pus, she would apply a fresh clean bandage. She always managed to nurture the open wounds back to health. Meanwhile, I waited anxiously to run again, even faster—creating still more wounds next to the previous ones, as the cycle continued. Ultimately, my knees got dreadfully scarred, reminding me of every past fall. I didn't care! I loved the excitement of running, the sound of the wind swishing past my ears, the sense of being in control, and the feeling of freedom!

> For I will restore health unto thee, and I will heal thee of thy wounds, saith the LORD… (Jeremiah 30:17)

Chapter 6

MAMAJI, CRAFT EXPERT AND CHEF

I am the LORD: that is my name: and my
glory will I not give to another, neither
my praise to graven images. (Isaiah 42:8)

The best part of living in Nairobi was visiting my grandmother's flat. The rest of my family began to teach me early on about my female role in Indian culture, but to my grandmother, cultural norms and traditions did not matter. She was partial to females—especially me! She favoured me by using every opportunity to shower me with gifts, even on my brother's birthdays. Her treatment of me was gentle and kind.

None were as special to me as my grandmother, Mamaji. Our love was mutual. Our firmly knit relationship made me want to spend time with her. I wanted to follow her and go wherever she went and do whatever she did. I thought that I would do anything for my grandmother.

At my grandmother's flat, I tried out her manual Singer sewing machine with the large floor foot-pedal. The thread would break, or the machine would jam, but that never mattered to her. She never got angry. She would fix the machine and have it ready for me to use on my next visit.

She had a huge metal trunk beside one wall which contained magnificent multi-coloured beads. These were left over from the times women would get together to embellish and decorate saris and Punjabi suits with paint or beads. At my request, she would carefully pour out some of her treasured beads into a bowl; I would sit cross-legged on the floor to thread them one by one or sew them onto cloth, just as she had trained me. She patiently taught me how to knit, and was always available to rescue my dropped stitches or unravel my mistakes. I learned quickly how tolerant she was.

As she sat on a chair near me, teasing me unmercifully, her hearty laughter would ring out as she watched me blush.

"Someday you are going to get married!" she would blurt in Punjabi.

"No! No!" I would politely answer, startled at her statement.

A burst of laughter would ring out of a mouth that framed crooked buck teeth. The laughter would get louder as she opened her mouth even wider. Her hair, set in a coconut-oil greased tight bun neatly fixed on the back of her head, was embellished with silver streaks. Her heavyset body was wrapped in a modest-coloured sari. I loved being near her warm body and feeling her tender arms around me. I knew that she loved me!

Gold bracelets adorned her strong arms. Her pierced nose held a heavy piece of gold jewelry. She had the longest ears I had ever seen. Heavy gold earrings deformed the holes in her dangling earlobes, making them even longer. Her forehead was small, and it framed squinting eyes. Old-fashioned glasses sometimes rested on her large nose. She was fairer than most Indian women, with milky velvety skin, except near the corners of her eyes, which wrinkled as she chuckled. She would never win a beauty contest, but I *loved* this woman. I loved her gentleness, her kindness, her warmth, her care, her laughter, her life…

On my frequent visits, I would indulge in favourite dishes made just for me. She had a keen sense of what I liked, and knew what my young palate would enjoy. My grandmother would make me tea brewed with milk and add copious amounts of sugar. I would gingerly pour it onto a saucer so the piping hot tea could cool down. I sipped it right from the saucer, just as she had taught me. Even if I accidentally spilled it, it would not matter to her. She knew I always wanted the end pieces of toast, lathered with a plentiful amount of fresh butter and jam. I would fold the bread in half, dip it in the warm tea, and savour the taste.

She knew intuitively what my favourite dishes were: *paranthas,* or fried flatbread sometimes filled with spiced mashed potatoes. Punjabi curry *pakora,* a curried soup with flavourful dumplings and rice. *Saag* and *maki-de-roti,* a ground spinach dish with cornflour *roti,* was the runner up. She would fondly prepare these dishes for me, and often!

What is ingrained in my memory is the fragrance of curry leaves and an assortment of spices arising from her gourmet kitchen as she prepared her specialties—all for me. She had skillfully perfected Indian food. Thinking about her dishes still makes my mouth water.

Sometimes, she would cut cubes of fresh, creamy dairy butter and roll them in sugar, and present them to me as treats. Then there was *malai,* which was prepared by boiling fresh whole milk bought daily from the dairy and skimming off the delectable cream that would settle on the top. After refrigeration, it would be served with a little sprinkling of sugar. This was by far the most delicious dessert I had ever eaten, and I have still not found one comparable! The secret ingredient in everything she made was *love*. Everything this dear, gentle woman did or made, I loved.

Venturing off to the dairy wasn't a chore—I constantly reminded myself that I would do *anything* for Mamaji. Inevitably,

I spent more time at my grandmother's home than my parents' place.

I would regularly accompany her to the Hindu temples. It was customary to leave our shoes, and anything made of leather or animal by-products, outside before entering. Animals were sacred, and were not to contaminate the temple.

We would pass the various shrines set up with idols and images of gods, goddesses, and animal gods. The form of worship was to offer food, vibrant-coloured flowers, money, or milk to the colourfully painted stone images. A gutter nearby would catch the milk poured out to the idols. A continuous flow of white creamy milk mixed with perfumed fresh flowers and burning incense sent off a sweet fragrance to the air. The experience of sights and smells was so captivating, it gave me the feeling that this must be divine.

At last, we would come to a room full of shiny brass bells of all sizes and shapes hanging from the ceiling. Excited, I wanted my grandmother to pick me up to ring as many bells as I could. I was amused and hypnotized by the sound, echoing and deafening.

At the end of the visit, the Hindu priests would distribute *parshad*, which had been prayed over and offered to the images of Hindu gods. It would consist of *sooji halwa*, made of cream of wheat fried in butter or oil, or a mixture of dried nuts, coconut, and raisins. I savoured the sweet tastes, consuming them with great delight! Returning home, I would look forward to our next visit together—just my grandmother and me.

> And this is life eternal, that they might know thee *the only true God, and Jesus Christ,* whom thou hast sent. (John 17:3, emphasis added)

Chapter 7

LIFE IN OUR FLAT

*…my people shall be satisfied
with my goodness…*
(Jeremiah 31:14, emphasis added)

Our second-floor flat was situated at one end of the building. Its five rooms included a washroom, a bathing room, the kitchen, a sitting room, and finally one large room at the end of a hallway where the whole family—my father, my mother, my older brother, and I—slept.

The narrow washroom had a sunken toilet in the floor with the accompanying water tank attached at the back wall. To flush, one had to pull a long chain. It was standing room only—or perhaps crouching room only. The small window high up on one wall allowed in some light. There were no sinks.

The large bathing room was empty except for a water tap attached halfway up the wall. A drain pierced the crude, unpolished concrete floor.

The screen-less windows in just about every room were rarely opened. This prevented the lizards crawling along the walls outside from entering, but it also kept the mid-afternoon heat out. The rooms were surprisingly cool from the cement walls, ceilings, and floors.

The kitchen on one side of the flat between the washroom and the bathing room had no appliances except for the small coal *githi* placed on the floor for cooking.

On first entering the room, one would notice on the only small counter a huge one-by-one-foot square box labelled Mischievous Biscuits, bought from a factory outlet. These biscuits were among the few store-bought items we enjoyed with our occasional afternoon tea, but they were especially reserved for guests. The box seemed so artificial and out of place. It was off limits to us children, as much as we may have wished to reach up and help ourselves to its contents. There it sat majestically, taking up a favoured place on the counter. On the front of the box was the printed image of a fat-faced child. It was the "mischievous kid" himself, who stared at me and almost taunted me for not being allowed to get a biscuit. I hated the image on the box, but loved the biscuits.

Vegetarian food was prepared from the fresh vegetables the local vendors would bring to our door daily, grown in the rich, fertile black fields nearby. My mother also cooked lentils or various types of beans for supper. My job was to pick rotten seeds or stones out of the dry lentils or rice, or to pluck off fragrant coriander leaves from their stems in preparation for the evening meals. Emptying pea pods was the most amusing. I worked alongside my mother, hearing only the sound of the snapping pods, revealing the plump, juicy sweet peas which lay neatly side by side. Some would somehow find their way into my mouth.

Hot *rotis* were our daily staple bread source, accompanied by homemade *dahi* or yogurt and mango or lime pickle. Curried vegetables, hot spicy lentils, or beans would simmer on the *githi* carefully placed in the centre of the floor, filling the kitchen with the aroma of fresh home-cooked Indian cuisine.

My mother was so focused on her work that she would not even notice my presence in the kitchen with her. I would watch as her purposeful hands created the evening meal from garden-fresh produce. With her black hair in a snug, perfectly pinned round bun covered with a light hair net, she kept her head down. I would try to get her attention so I could taste the concoction she was making. At times, I would be offered a small bowl of soup, with the expectation that I would find a place on the floor, well out of the way. Savouring each spice and herb that contributed to the mouth-watering broth, I never complimented my mother—I simply never knew how.

I wished I could enter her world, but somehow there was an imaginary stone barrier around her that seemed impenetrable. The wall was so high, I could not climb it to get to the other side. I wanted her recognition for something—*anything*. I wanted her to acknowledge that I was alive, but silently she worked, oblivious to my presence, betraying little emotion.

At mealtime, we would quietly sit cross-legged on the clean concrete floor, or on small wooden stools placed in a circle. We would break apart pieces of roti smothered in fresh ghee, folding and scooping up the delicious curry with the accompanying fragrant basmati rice. Sometimes the food would be washed down with a yogurt drink called *lassi*. It was a fulfilling meal worth waiting for.

The vendors also brought all kinds of freshly picked aromatic fruit to our doorstep—papayas, many types of mangoes, various passion fruits, different sizes and types of bananas, guavas, pineapples, and some exotic fruits I could not name.

On special occasions, this paradise of fruit would be replaced by delectable Indian desserts bought from a specialty dessert shop. Everyone's favourite was *rusgulla*, creamy white cheese curd balls cooked in a thin sugar syrup and later infused with rose water. *Gulab jamun* were fried flour and *khoya* (a dried byproduct of milk), spiced with cardamom and placed in a thick sugary syrup.

Barfi, a cheesy white pistachio fudge overlaid with a garnish of thin silver edible foil sheets called *vark*, was also a favourite.

Simple curtains adorned the metal-framed window in the sitting room, which was spacious, but smaller than the bedroom. It had two sofas, a centre table, and a small bar fridge against one wall. The fridge stored the essentials—milk, butter, and homemade ice-cream—in an ice tray. It was a prized piece of furniture that was off limits to children: it had a pure white exterior and immaculately clean interior, and was expected to stay that way, dent- and mark-free.

We were not allowed to sit on the sofa except in the presence of company. The hard brown leather never softened with the years. I did not know how to sit on it. Was I to sit back and allow my legs to dangle? I tried to look as graceful as possible, so I decided to sit on the edge of the couch to match the grown-ups, my legs barely touching the floor. Expected to be seen and not heard, I sat submissively listening to adult gibberish. I was never asked to participate in any conversations. I was never asked any questions or given any opportunity to state my opinions or comments. It was easy—all I had to do was sit and listen—but boring.

Sometimes I would be asked to carry a tray of glasses full of "squash" for visitors. I would walk gingerly to keep it level, as I knew the consequences of dropping it. Not only would it be an embarrassment for my family, but it would lead especially to trouble for me. My own mother would be sure to yell at me with words I was too young to understand.

The spacious bedroom at one end of the flat had a large bed. I slept in between my parents, while my brother had his own cot placed against the wall on the opposite end of the room. During the day, this large bed was also used to spread out dry laundry, just brought in from the clothesline outside. I would fold each piece with my little fingers. No conversation was ever made with my mother as we worked silently side by side. I could not fold as perfectly as she could, but watched intently, trying to copy her as flawlessly as possible, hoping to please her. Sometimes she would suddenly leave me alone to attend the front door. I couldn't help thinking that I could better spend my time playing outside with other children, rather than just folding laundry all by myself.

At other times, my mother would step away to check on the food cooking in the kitchen. Once again, I would be left to complete the job of endlessly folding garments. At times she would call me names, the meanings of which I never knew. These words were so familiar that they never bothered me. *They are only used for me, so they must be special,* I thought. But I did not *feel* special.

Sometimes, I would be instructed to lie on my brother's cot for an afternoon nap. I never slept; rather, I rolled from side to side, only to be impeccably still if my mother walked in. If I didn't pretend that I was sleeping, I would receive a severe scolding. I *wanted* to fall asleep to make my mother happy. But staring at the sparse furniture, the space, and the floor, I felt confined and alone.

The room had a polished, painted, burgundy cement floor which was always spotless and glossy. It was here that I would sit obediently as my mother prepared to read her religious book, the *Gita*, which was carefully balanced on an open sandalwood stand on the floor. With her hands at each side of the book, her pursed lips would tighten before she started. Cross-legged on the cold hard floor, she never fidgeted. Reading in a solemn monotone, there was little sentiment or passion as words poured out continuously from dry parched lips. She hardly stopped to take a breath, but would occasionally swallow the spit that accumulated in her mouth. Sometimes an echo would accompany her reading in the bare room.

But what stirred up fear and bewilderment in my childlike mind were the pictures she would show me from her religious books. I would sit, gripped with horror, as I studied images like those out of a comic strip, outlined in black and filled in with colours. I saw hideous creatures carrying pitchforks and torturing people. I saw pictures of them burning people in huge black cauldrons. I tried to understand what the humans could have possibly done to deserve such punishment. "This is what will happen to you if you don't follow the gods," she would add sternly in Punjabi. I would be terrified, but stayed still, as I had learned early to hide my emotions. I didn't expect to be comforted.

On closing the book, my mother expected me to accompany her prayer reciting. I followed her voice and filled the room with resonance as we sang memorized chants in unison. We would meet the next day, sitting on the same barren floor, following the same ritual, as I dutifully sat and listened. I would gaze at the people in her book once again, perceiving faces of panic and fright. Their looks of suffering as they were tortured by revolting, ugly creatures startled me. Again, I sat in shock as I tried to comprehend what I was seeing in my little five-year-old mind.

There was a cupboard in the corner of the bedroom with a round tin container, which once housed delicious hard toffees from England, but was now used to accumulate money—*my* money. This was cash that had been given to me by relatives at various celebratory occasions over the years. The tin was placed on a shelf high out of my reach, and was only brought down to be added to each time a relative handed me money. Routinely, I was sternly asked to hand over the cash after they left so it could be deposited in this colourful tin box with the plastic hands of a clock on the lid. Once again, it would be carefully placed out of reach of my small hands.

One day, the tin box was taken down to my surprise, with no reason given. It was now full of bills and coins. I remember the distress I felt as I watched my mother remove all the money. I was confused: I had carefully saved what belonged to me, but now it was no longer mine. I began to cry and plead for my box of money. It had been given to me, but was now empty! I no longer cared for the plastic clock hands on the front lid, and tried bending them off in anger and disgust, trying to make sense of what just happened. Despite my anguish, no explanation was given for how the money was to be spent. I felt betrayed, as I had thought that the contents belonged to *me*.

After this event, I no longer wanted to store away anything I valued, as I knew it would be taken away. Even when I was given some rolls of Maynard's gel candy that someone brought over from England, I thought it necessary to indulge in all of them right away instead of saving them. Crawling under the bed, I ate them all. *I am not going to have these taken from me too,* I thought. I got so sick that I began to have nightmares of huge marshmallow-type objects trying to suffocate me. To this day, I still refuse any candy that reminds me of these wine gels! No one knew why I was so sick, and didn't seem to connect the situation to the candies that were suddenly missing.

Any money handed to me by a relative in the future was promptly and obediently passed on to my mother after their visit. Now that the tin container was gone, I had little that belonged to *me*, and no longer had much regard for money anyway.

I was forced to absorb injustices from a world that often put me aside, taught me to be inexpressive, and forced me to internalize the hurts, confusion, and loneliness which haunted me.

Although incapable of expressing my feelings in words and unable to make sense of them at my young age, as I got older, my understanding grew. My sensitivity toward the surroundings and the environment in which I was both an observer and a participant was well beyond my age.

It was culturally expected for me to perform household duties as a female. I had no hobbies and no interests. Household chores didn't elicit gratitude or praise—they were to be done as an act of duty. But I did long for words of affirmation from one person in particular: my mother. The result of this treatment was that I felt I had no value.

I lived in fear of being reprimanded and scolded—for making childlike mistakes. I didn't mind helping my mother if I could be close to her, yearning for a relationship. Instead, my mother remained emotionally distant, and lacked the essential emotion of love towards me. I wanted her to talk to me, notice me, touch me, and caress me as *her child*, but it *never* happened. She was unwilling to share her thoughts, perhaps afraid to make herself vulnerable, reveal her emotions, or show any of her weakness. She remained stern and cold for the rest of my upbringing.

My mother did not realize the effect she was having on me by repeatedly taking my gift money—*my possession*. Without an explanation to help me understand, her actions provoked me to anger and made me want to hoard things. This made me lose confidence in my mother, and opened me up to feelings of sadness and lack of self-worth.

O send out *thy light* and *thy truth:* let them lead me; let them bring me unto thy holy hill, and to thy tabernacles. (Psalm 43:3, emphasis added)

Chapter 8

LADIES' AFTERNOON *SATSUNG*

God is a Spirit: and they that worship him
must worship him *in spirit and in truth.*
(John 4:24, emphasis added)

I routinely accompanied my mother to the ladies' *satsung*, a time of singing and reading out of Hindu religious books. Sitting cross-legged on the floor, heads covered with the end of their saris, everyone jammed into one of the ladies' living rooms, the women, dressed in sombre colours, looked *religious*. My mother, chosen by the women to read out of the same book she read to me privately, would sit on the floor much like at home, but this time in a prominent position at the front of the room for all to see and hear. She looked pious and occupied. I had a sense of respect for her, thinking, *Everyone is looking at my mom!*

At first the room had an atmosphere of mournful stillness, cut through when the women broke into devotional song and music. The mood now lightened, charmed by the sound of the *tolki*, a small Indian drum laid on its side, hitting one's bare hands on each end to produce a rhythm. I would mimic this action in private on my lap with both hands, pretending I was holding the drum, as I was not allowed to touch the sacred instruments.

A floor accordion called a harmonium kept the music lively, loud, and spellbinding. Sometimes a woman sombrely hit a tambourine to keep the tempo consistent with the rest of the music. Melodious, monotonous, and almost addictive sounds filled the room, accompanied by the singing and chanting of the women.

At the end of the service, *parshad,* a delicacy consisting of nuts, dried coconut, dried prunes, raisins, and almonds, which had first been prayed over and offered to idols, was passed around for all to partake.

Sitting, watching, and listening at the *satsung* appealed to my physical senses: a friendly crowd of women assembled together; the calming, monotonous, repetitive music that almost hypnotized me; and the delicious *parshad* distributed at the end of the ceremony. My senses were tantalized by the delightful sound, smell, and taste.

I was not sure of the intended effect, but leaving the women's sing did not make me feel any holier or purer. I didn't feel any closer to the gods. It was just something I was required to participate in, but the musical instruments did intrigue my curiosity.

But the LORD is the true God, he is the living God, and an everlasting king... (Jeremiah 10:10)

Chapter 9

THE RED DOUBLE-DECKER BUS

...thou hast covered me in my
mother's womb. I will praise thee; for
I am fearfully and wonderfully made:
marvellous are thy works...
(Psalm 139:13–14)

Car trips were rare; like the rest of the people in the courtyard, my parents did not own a vehicle. My Uncle Aahan owned a red Volkswagen, which my brother and I liked to sit inside and pretend we were driving; we would also sometimes clean it for him. Our most frequent car trips were to the airport to drop off or pick up my uncle, heading to or returning from the UK for his military service. My grandfather owned a jeep which he once used to take my brother and me to another city, where he dropped us off to have our tonsils removed. It was traumatic for me to be left alone in a hospital ward with many other children. It made me stay close to my brother until we returned home.

Most often, we travelled by a British red double-decker bus for visits to the doctor, or on short shopping excursions accompanying my mother. These outings only lasted for the afternoon, and were devoid of conversation. My mother would hold my hand stiffly as we boarded and exited the bus, or when it was necessary to cross the street. I could never understand why it was essential for her to squeeze my hand so tightly. I would not wander off or run away, and would do as I was told, so why did she hang on so tightly? Hers was the touch I longed for, but this was an urgent quick crush of the hand, a harsh reminder of the hold's purpose: to prevent me being hit by a vehicle. In short, this hand holding just felt like the required *duty* of a parent. Again, silence… I didn't know where we were going until I was hauled into the dreaded doctor's office.

These visits to the doctor's office were pitiless. He routinely pushed my tongue down with a cold, metal tongue depressor that had been soaked in a bitter disinfectant. Gagging with my eyes bulging out, I wondered what he was looking for.

Next, I was to lie on the firm black bed and wait for the next procedure in the unfriendly dark office. Suddenly, someone would step into the room, most likely the doctor. Without warning or preparation, my underpants would be pulled down firmly, and I would receive the usual piercing needle jab in my buttocks. Left alone to console myself, I would sob, the echo of my cries filling the strange-smelling room.

We usually left for home abruptly, but on some occasions, we would stop at a fabric shop first. Here my mother would purchase cloth used to make my home-made dresses: plain pastel-coloured cotton frocks, or some with geometric patterns and matching hair ribbons. Sometimes I would be allowed to choose sparkling glass bangles before we left for home. Purposely lingering, I took my time so we could stay longer in the brightly coloured shop with its exotic saris and Punjabi suits. Our hurried trip back home was always in silence.

I did not have the relationship with my mother for which I yearned. I was impoverished when it came to human contact; I longed to have my hands squeezed lovingly, to be given a warm embrace, or a soft kiss placed on my cheek. I wanted a mother who cared and loved me. I craved the human touch of love. I wanted to feel *worth* and *value*.

> Can a woman forget her sucking child, that she should not have compassion on the son of her womb? yea, they may forget, *yet will I not forget thee. Behold, I have graven thee upon the palms of my hands...* (Isaiah 49:15–16, emphasis added)

Chapter 10

PREPARATION FOR SCHOOL

For *the hurt of the daughter* of
my people am *I hurt*…
(Jeremiah 8:21, emphasis added)

The Catholic primary school I attended in Nairobi was managed and operated by nuns. We were each given a yellow plastic rosary, which I used to chant the names of Hindu gods, just like I was taught at home.

It was a large concrete building with a row of rooms which opened to the outside. I remember the huge grassy yard where we ran and played was bordered by a large chain link metal fence.

The highlight of each day was when a vendor would wander into the school yard to sell spicy round *pakoras* made from mashed potatoes deep fried in a coating of chickpea flour batter; no longer warm, but were still delicious. I was allowed on occasion to purchase one of these mouth-watering appetizers at recess time. My mouth burning from the bite of the chilies, I would wonder why I liked them so much!

The school uniform was a pale aqua dress with a stiff white collar and a dark maroon sweater. The daily preparation for school included my mother combing my long black hair and then braiding it. It seemed pointless to me, but she struggled to remove every single one of the many tangles. The two braids, looped tightly to the sides of my head with ribbons, made my head ache. The cheerfully bright colours of these ribbons would be the only consolation after the dreaded procedure was completed each morning. With my head throbbing from the pulling and stretching necessary to make a neat hairdo, I did not dare rebel against my mother's work of art. I stayed quiet, forcing back tears.

What sometimes followed was the customary nail-cutting service. As the clipper approached my nails, I would cringe like a hurt animal. As the cutter clipped away past the whites of the nail, I held my breath. I was sure nails were not meant to be cut so short, but a few moans were all I managed to spill out. I sometimes tried to pull away, but my hand would be held tighter, so I surrendered to a force greater than mine. *I will hold my breath,* I thought, *it may ease the pain.* It was like my mother was at *war* with my nails, blaming them for growing too quickly.

After the practice ended, I would cautiously and carefully curl my fists, encapsulating the sensitive tips to protect them from further harm. The finale was a barrage of words flying out of my mother's mouth like a foreign language. I could not fathom the names used by my mother in her haste and frustration as she attended to my care. I felt like I was interfering in her busy schedule, so I had better cooperate. There was always a sense of urgency. There was no physical contact with me except what was compulsory. The goal seemed to be for the least expanse of skin to be touched with the least amount of tenderness. I felt like an object that must remain silent. Unable to communicate, I remained confused, but was pleased once the ordeal was over—for the time being.

As a serious and a quiet child, taking in everything happening around me and to me, I was trying to assimilate and adjust. I was the unwanted child. I was the unloved child—a *girl!* I was the girl who held no value to the family, except to my grandmother.

In preparation for school, I had to learn that I would not be handled adoringly and kindly. My mother's lack of affectionate touch gave me the sense that parts of my body were supposed to be foreign to me and did not deserve respect or careful care. Everything done for me was out of duty: suddenly and grudgingly, while vile words were flung at me, instead of the terms of endearment which I so needed.

What I desired as a child was a warm caress, a loving look, a compliment, or a meaningful touch that would make me feel valued and loved. I hungered for *love*—but life went on without it. I began to feel insignificant and neglected.

> ...the *meekness and gentleness* of Christ... (2 Corinthians 10:1, emphasis added)

> Take my yoke upon you, and learn of me; for *I am meek and lowly* in heart: and ye shall find *rest unto your souls.* (Matthew 11:29, emphasis added)

Chapter 11

SIBLING RIVALRY

For all have sinned, and come short
of the glory of God…
(Romans 3:23)

My mother and her family were born and lived in a village in Punjab, India. Her growing up years were spent with her maternal grandparents, for reasons I do not know. When her father moved to Kenya to look for a job to support the family, he sent for them a few years later to join him.

The personality disparity between my maternal grandparents was dramatic. While my grandmother was calm, thoughtful, and compassionate, my grandfather was the very opposite. His work with hardened prisoners as a warden in a jungle made him highly respected but also feared by those who knew him. His violent and spontaneous temper often made him lose friends who had been forced to bow to his demands. He ruled his household with an iron fist of hatred, authority, and prejudice. He chose favourites among his children based on their gender, success, and good looks.

Reena, one of my mother's two sisters, was the preferred daughter, fairer and more educated than the others. She always wore two perfect braids neatly tied at the ends with a colourful ribbon, adorning the sides of her light, oblong, serious face. I never saw her smile. She was allowed to attend secretarial school. The stenography she learned enabled her brag to everyone about her "short-hand" abilities. At times, she would take me aside to patiently teach me the simple word symbols. Her obsessive-compulsive behaviour about neatness became quite fascinating to me as I inquisitively watched her strange and repetitive gestures from a distance. The sheet over her prized trunk of clothes was repetitively corrected so many times, I would wonder what she was trying to align it with. Even though I did not understand her queer behaviour, I liked being with her. My mother did not have a close relationship with this sister.

My mother's younger sister, Alka, even though she was darker than Reena, was liked by everyone because of her laid-back and happy nature. She completed a clerical college program as well. She always sported western dresses. I enjoyed her company, especially when she would braid my hair without hurting me.

People, especially my maternal grandfather, often compared my two uncles. The older of the two, Aahan, was fairer, had superior grades in school, and excelled in athletics. He ended up in the British military, which moved him even higher in the eyes of the family and the community, and especially after being decorated in his military service by the president of the country. He had a charismatic personality, receiving the attention and admiration of all who conversed with him.

The younger brother, Bulus, with his irregular buck teeth and very dark skin, was not esteemed by his father. He was not accomplished in school, nor did he win any sports awards. His embarrassingly loud, rough voice and awkward laughter often exposed his uncultured mannerisms and behaviour.

My mother, the oldest of the five children, was the least favoured. Her darker complexion was considered unattractive by community standards. Although she was uneducated, she was talented in crocheting, sewing, knitting, and embroidery. Even though her handmade projects were the envy of her friends, these skills and artifacts held little value or meaning to her.

My mother never smiled, and I never saw her happy. She had to accept her lower place as a woman, usurped in rank by her younger brother, Aahan. At the time she was growing up, it was customary for females to be taken out of school prematurely to help with household chores and responsibilities in the home and eventually to be married off in an arranged marriage. Unlike her sisters, she was forced to leave school and perform household duties. She also received the verbal abuse of her father, as did her younger brother, Bulus.

As I was growing up, from fragments of what I heard, my mother complained about her father's insults and lack of regard for her. To be degraded by him and put in a lower position in front of everyone must have been devasting and dishonouring for my mother. This partiality and favouritism in my mother's family created divisions between siblings, ruining their relationships, which never healed even into adulthood.

I knew my mother carried a lot of animosity toward her siblings, prompted by jealousy and envy and fuelled by her sisters and brother being more favoured and privileged than her. It caused her to be encased in a cocoon of sorrow, bitterness, self-pity, and self-absorption. She seemed hostile towards her younger two sisters, who enjoyed more freedom than she did.

Puzzled by my mother's ominous behaviour, I wondered what additional hidden abuses and hurts must she have suffered. What torments did she experience in her life that she had to suffer privately, unable to share with those around her? What must it have been like to be controlled in every aspect of her life? Even as an adult, her destiny relating to career or husband had all been decided by her parents, and she did not have a say in the decision-making process.

I was never sure what would set my mother off in anger or make her act against me. This made me fear her. Nevertheless, I still hungered for her approval, her love, her attention—her touch, the touch I thought should be expected of a *mother*.

However, I never wanted to follow my mother's example in my life! I could never remember my mother smiling or laughing or being happy. She always looked miserable. The world was her enemy—especially anyone responsible for making her unhappy. I found her hatred towards others repulsive. She would lash out unreasonably, even at me, her own child, whom she treated like a scapegoat. The older I got, the more I started to see my mother as a hurting soul. I wanted to be a ray of sunshine and love to her, but instead I turned out to be a dark cloud in her life.

My mother never recovered from her ill treatment by her father, but she also never tried to break the cycle she found herself in. I saw so much of my grandfather's harsh spirit developing in my mother. Sadly, I never recognized any of my grandmother's qualities of love, kindness, gentleness, and sensitivity in her.

I wanted to feel the same kind of respect and love I had for my grandmother towards my mother. I felt sorry for her, but it was difficult as she never responded to me.

Even though I loved being with the family, there were times going to Mamaji's house gave me a sense of anguish. What I had thought was a perfect family was not so perfect after all. I felt sorry for the treatment my younger uncle, Bulus, got from my grandfather. He never measured up in his father's eyes. He was never good enough at anything he did. I overheard how this uncle had been beaten by my grandfather on occasion—apparently with a slipper. After some of these occurrences, I recognized something was gravely wrong in the atmosphere in that home. I somehow knew my uncle was the victim, needing consoling, so I would try to encourage him to play games with me.

I remember one such occasion when my Uncle Bulus had been beaten quite badly and there was nothing I could do to cheer him. The picture of him broken in spirit—sitting in their living room, staring into space, and looking sad—stayed fixed in my memory. I heard my Aunt Alka saying in the background that he had sustained bruises. I remember my heart aching for him. I began to fear my grandfather, even though he never hurt me.

My mother and father were married through an arrangement made by their parents. They first saw each other on the night of their wedding in India. It was expected that they would work through their differences and live with the commitment of marriage. It was a rocky start as they tried to make a home with limited funds while tolerating and accepting an abusive relationship with her father.

The circle of partiality my mother experienced poisoned even our home. My older brother had already been enjoying the special treatment of our parents for four years before I came along. He won continuous privileges from my parents, being the revered *male*! Due to cultural norms, I grew up in his shadow, and little affection was demonstrated to me by my parents. I felt covetous and envious of the position he held in their eyes. He could do no wrong—even when he dumped a whole bottle of Coca-Cola on my head, he got away with it!

My brother's birthday celebrations were bigger and more auspicious than mine. Delicious English pastries topped with buttercream icing bought from the bakery were often displayed and consumed with enjoyment as the radio played a "Happy Birthday" song, announcing my brother by name. I began to feel he was better than me, but at the same time I was becoming increasingly aware of my neglect and being put aside in deference to my brother.

One time, my dad and Uncle Aahan tricked me in believing they were staying at home, but I saw them get into his car with my brother and drive off to watch a movie at the cinema. It was a war movie, I was told later, but I still felt excluded! I could never understand why I was not part of their trips and why my brother was so honoured.

My heart hurt. I had to learn, adjust, and accept this was the reality for a *girl!*

> For the wages of sin is death; but *the gift of God is eternal life through Jesus Christ our Lord.* (Romans 6:23, emphasis added)

Chapter 12

DAD LEAVES FOR A FOREIGN LAND

*When my father and my mother forsake
me, then the LORD will take me up.*
(Psalm 27:10, emphasis added)

Dad was born in a small village in Punjab, Northern India. He was the middle child of three brothers and two sisters. He was well-liked because of his gentle, soft-spoken nature.

As a student living and growing up in India, he once came across an old man, a *guru* who my dad claims saved him from the attack of a cobra. Apparently, this cobra would repeatedly follow him into the secluded spot in the forest where my dad would spend hours studying. After many days, it eventually tried to hypnotize him, preparing to strike, when this guru somehow suddenly intervened, and saved my dad's life by alerting him and forcing him to leave his favourite study spot. My dad felt forever indebted to this guru-friend, who promised him that he would return reincarnated as my dad's future son and would take care of him till the end of his life.

After this man's death, my dad believed without a shadow of doubt that my brother was the reincarnated guru. Watching my brother's mannerisms and behaviour, he tried to convince himself of this fact. The only supporting evidence was how he neatly folded an electrical cord! I had also done the same thing, but it went unnoticed. Many of the privileges given to my brother seemed to be repayment for my dad's life. My brother could do no wrong in my parents' eyes, but if you ask me, my brother was *no saint!*

Dad had a slender build when he was first married, due to his impoverished upbringing in India. After getting married and moving to Kenya, he erupted into a heavy three-hundred-pound man. He was hardworking and devoted to the family. He had no hobbies.

Being 5'11" didn't give him presence when he entered a room, as he was a humble man. He wore a black Hitler-style moustache that sat neatly trimmed under his prominent nose, which a pair of thick black-framed Groucho Marx glasses made appear shorter. His jet-black hair, thickly placed on his head, was a stark contrast to his fair skin. A large black beauty spot adorned one cheek. People called him "handsome" mainly because he was fair.

On one of his strong hands was a blue-grey tattoo of the sign "OM." He never explained the meaning of it, but it was a Hindu chant word. He wore a huge gold ring with an inset square red ruby stone on his ring finger, according to the advice of a well-meaning soothsayer. It was supposed to improve his fortunes and allow him to be prosperous.

On his last trip to India, some gurus, reading some old documents supposedly written hundreds of years before his visit, foretold of the millions he would make in a foreign land. He believed this with a passion and looked forward to when it would come to pass. Perhaps this was the destiny he was seeking: fortune and success.

Dad was well-respected by the Indian community in Nairobi. Some told him that he had the gift of palmistry—reading palms and foretelling the future. After reading his own palm, he concluded he would attain great fortune in a foreign land. Everyone else shared their own personal stories to support the accuracy of his predictions.

The only close contact I remember having with my dad in Kenya was on a fateful day when I was summoned to sit on the hard, burgundy couch in the sitting room while he had a talk with me. My mother would enter, exit, and then re-enter the room, waiting for the verdict of "guilty" being handed down and judgement pronounced for my "crime." *Some* critical event had occurred which annoyed them both as they tried to get a confession out of me.

My dad looked mad: his front teeth forcefully curling his lower lip inward as he bit down hard. It looked painful! The whites around his large black eyes showed more than they should have, popping out of his head as they stared with repugnance, trying to pierce and pry. His eyes got more fearsome, trying to unfold my guilt. For the first time, I sat watching my dad, trying to understand why he was so fixated on me. I couldn't make sense of it!

"Tell me what it means," he kept repeating in Punjabi. "Do you know the meaning of what you said?" I had never been aware that there were any words I was never supposed to repeat. The kids in the courtyard were older than me, and I must have picked up their derogatory language, or perhaps even repeated what my mother would say to me. I assured my dad in my childlike way that I did not know what he was talking about. I *didn't!* It was the first time in my life that I feared Dad. I was left confused, trying to understand the reason for the scolding, and was told never to repeat the words again. I wasn't even sure which words they meant!

Dad, the storyteller, never tired of intriguing his audience— often with the same stories, voiced with the same expression, with the same familiar ending executed so cleverly; he was able to deliver the final punch line and get the desired reaction of laughter and surprise *each time!* It always seemed like a fresh new story, conveyed with the same emotion as the first time anyone had ever heard it. Everyone who visited would be mesmerized by his talent, listening for hours as Dad entertained them.

I remember the few times he would tell us the same fictitious stories. Why, I wondered, was the story of Ali Baba and the Forty Thieves so fascinating to him? The only part I liked was the magical door that opened at the words, "Open Sesame!" Why would I want to learn about some thieves who hid their stolen treasure for Ali Baba to eventually find? I could never understand the moral lessons behind them, but he must have enjoyed our steady gaze as we listened in fascination. At that time, Dad told us few stories of his childhood in India; more importantly, he never shared why he was moving to Canada.

One day, all the furniture was moved out of the sitting room in preparation for a religious ceremony to be performed by orange-clad Hindu priests. Invited guests with family and friends crowded the room. Everyone sat on the floor. The ritual was necessary for my dad to have a successful trip to Canada. It seemed to go on for hours and hours into the evening. I did not understand what the commotion was all about. So many people, so many well-wishers, but why? No one explained to me that my dad was going to a far-away country.

I did not miss my dad when he left for Canada. I was not close to him, as he hardly spent time with me.

...I will receive you. And will be a Father unto you, and ye shall be *my sons and daughters,* saith the Lord Almighty. (2 Corinthians 6:17–18, emphasis added)

Chapter 13

NECESSARY HAIR RITUAL

*...even the very hairs of your head are all
numbered. Fear not therefore: ye are of
more value than many sparrows.*
(Luke 12:7)

My secure, comfortable loving life with my grandmother got altered abruptly as my mother, my brother, and I were to also immigrate to Winnipeg, Manitoba, Canada to join my dad. I was seven years old.

Nobody explained that we would never return to Kenya, or that I would *never* see my grandmother again. I hardly knew the word "Canada," but for others, excitement filled the air as relatives prepared to send us off to this far-away place.

Firstly, certain things had to be taken care of. I heard that my hair would need to be cut to live in Canada. I was not sure why it was necessary, but everyone said it would make life easier there.

One day, fooled into believing we were going for ice cream cones, I was instead whisked off to the barber shop. This must have been the only way I would agree to go along. I remember crying in shock as I fought to keep my hair. They tried to convince me it was very necessary to go to this foreign land. But I thought it must be a *horrible* place if it required giving up my hair.

My Uncle Aahan started the "fire" by giving the reasons for the haircut, while my mother fanned it with her insistent reasons for this necessary ritual. Apparently, my uncle hated long hair. There was no consoling me; I refused to believe my hair had to go. I sensed that part of me was now gone, and I felt ashamed as they tried to replace my lost hair with ice cream! Suddenly ice cream, a rare treat, was not so delightful anymore. I would rather have had my hair!

The next morning, I felt a sense of humiliation and emptiness as I tried to reason through what had happened. My body had been invaded without my consent. I could not understand why my mother was allowed to keep *her* long hair. It did not make any sense.

My Aunt Alka came over and appeared to be concerned about my reaction the night before. She tried to convince me how modern and pretty I looked, and how no one had long hair in this new land. I did not believe her, and did not want to trust anyone anymore.

As a child, I was so upset and confused at an event as minor as my first haircut. Something had been taken away from me once again, without my knowledge or consent or a good enough explanation.

Regardless of what the adults thought—they were doing what they thought would prepare me for a foreign country—in my eyes, I had been deceived by those I was supposed to trust. Also, this invasion of my privacy led me to feel insecure and defenseless. The event was the beginning of a journey with many more bumps.

LORD, thou hast *heard the desire of the humble:* thou wilt prepare their heart, thou wilt cause thine ear to hear... (Psalm 10:17, emphasis added)

Chapter 14

LEAVING NAIROBI, KENYA

...I bare you on eagles' wings, and
brought you unto myself.
(Exodus 19:4, emphasis added)

My only experience of travelling to the Nairobi Airport
had been to pick up my Uncle Aahan when he returned
from overseas military training. Various people in the party
accompanying our family placed garlands of fragrant flowers around
his neck to welcome and honour him for his accomplishments, as
photographs were taken to mark the auspicious occasion. Most of
my personal memories were of nausea from the car ride.

This next visit to the airport was different. I was given a new
red coat to wear—something I had never seen nor worn before.
After our brief goodbyes, my mother, my brother Sohna, and I
walked away from our relatives to the other side of the gate. We
were leaving Nairobi, Kenya, and I did not know why!

As we sat in the airplane, buckled in tight, I felt trapped in its
confines. When the evening meal was served, my mother forbade
us to eat anything for fear of being poisoned. Sleeping upright
through the night, I was awoken in the morning by the sound of
a food tray placed before me. Despite our hunger, we were *still*
not allowed to eat, but my brother reminded my mother that we

were starving. I waited for her to let me try the large, half-cut pink fruit on my tray. I had never seen nor tasted this fruit, but the colour looked appealing, especially the red cherry in the centre. I was ready to eat anything to ease the pangs of hunger, but the bitterly sour flavour was the worst thing I had ever tasted in my life. Leaving it behind, I ate the sweet, candied cherry.

Suddenly, I had a queasy feeling in my stomach. I glanced out the window, noticing the large body of water below; without warning, I deposited the little I had in my stomach onto my new red coat. My mother, both irritated and embarrassed, wiped my coat with the aid of a uniformed flight attendant. The rest of the trip was even more uncomfortable for me, knowing I had ruined my coat and made my mother angry; besides that, I had to put up with the sickening odour coming off it.

Sohna remained quiet as my mother repeatedly warned us of this new country: how we must stay together and not eat *anything* for fear of being *poisoned*.

Landing in Athens, Greece, then Paris, France for a short stop-over, we were supposed to change flights, but the announcement for our next boarding was in French. Sohna, eleven years old, asked two powder-blue uniformed attendants behind a desk which gate would take us to our destination: Winnipeg, Manitoba, Canada. With some linguistic difficulty, they somehow managed to inform him that unfortunately we had missed the flight. They booked us a room in the airport for an overnight stay to board the next flight out in the morning for Winnipeg.

In the meantime, several food vouchers were given to each of us for complete meals. Still, my mother insisted we should not eat any food we did not recognize, even though my brother and I were famished and complaining. From her carry-on, she magically took out a small box of *pera,* a sweet, round, beige-coloured Indian fudge, probably given to us by a relative at the Nairobi Airport as a farewell gift. These treats and the Coca-Cola which we got free from the vouchers—the only sustenance available at the airport that we recognized—were the only things we were allowed to consume.

The rest of the evening was spent running up and down the nearby two-way escalators, never having seen *moving stairs* before. Like a bunch of wild monkeys, we continued to chase each other up and down, as my mother looked on, scolding us to stop.

With gnawing hunger pains and empty stomachs, we entered our hotel room at the end of the day. From the window in the tiny room, we could see the gigantic planes on the tarmac, billowing out engine noises and vibrations we felt all night. Icy air blew on us throughout the entire night from an air conditioning unit, which was foreign to us; we had no idea how to adjust it. All three of us lay on the tiny bed in our clothes, trying to get some rest in the cold room. What seemed odd to me were the numerous neatly placed towels of various sizes hanging in the bathroom. I had also never seen a bathtub before.

The next morning, after we washed by running the tap in the tub—not knowing there was a shower overhead or how to use it— we left without using the food vouchers given to us for breakfast. We boarded a plane leaving for Winnipeg.

We were glad to see my dad waiting for us at the airport with Uncle Bulus, who had moved to Canada shortly before him. The first thing we announced to my dad was how our mother had not allowed us to eat on our trip for fear of being poisoned. My dad turned to my mother, distressed that she had prohibited us from using the vouchers and not allowed us to eat for three days!

I was not too excited about this new place. It was strange, cold, and barren. Where were the sunshine and the open fields? Most of all, where was my *grandmother*?

In trying to understand my mother, I was confused by her insecure behaviour. In our trip to Canada, she seemed to trust no one for fear of being poisoned. Although seemingly illogical for a woman in her thirties, she had never traveled alone; perhaps she was overwhelmed with fear due to a lack of understanding the English language, and the prospect of facing new places and people.

Ignorance of a western country's ways made necessary adjustments and acceptance even more difficult. Learning about a new culture was a daunting task for each of us, and each of us experienced it in our own way.

This was a new chapter in my life.

...I am with thee, and will keep thee in all places whither thou goest... (Genesis 28:15, emphasis added)

Chapter 15

WINNIPEG, MANITOBA

God looked down from heaven upon the
children of men, to see if there were any
that did understand, that did seek God.
(Psalm 53:2)

Settling in St. Boniface, a neighbourhood in Winnipeg, was a new experience. Our apartment was located on the lower level of one of the many rickety two-story rowhouses that stretched the length of the street. When entering the front door of the dingy old building, every step creaked. The building was poorly lit, and smelled of rancid wood and cigarette smoke—an instant reminder of its decay.

Inside the apartment, the rooms were lined up along a corridor. The shared bathroom was outside the apartment, and available for the use of all the building's tenants.

Although my dad had settled a few years ahead of us, my parents were preoccupied with their many adjustments and adaptations to this new country: its different dress code, various customs, and strange people. I stayed out of their way, trying to accept this bizarre place on my own, with its brisk and cold winds, dead trees, brown grass, and concrete sidewalks. I found its people unsympathetic, unfriendly, and inquisitive.

Our family went for a walk one evening, very much like we had often done in Kenya. As we ventured down the sidewalk, we noticed people coming out of their homes to watch us foreigners with curiosity. They stared without comment as we paraded by, but we could almost hear their thoughts: "Look at that dark-skinned family of four. Look at the strangely dressed woman with a red dot on her forehead, and her long-braided hair."

We were obviously peculiar to the people in this French community.

Returning home from one of these walks, my embarrassed dad demanded that my mother never wear a sari again. He wanted her to wear pants, just like everyone else in this country. She was told to cut her hair short to fit in (although she actually kept it long for years afterward). She was not to wear a *bindi*—the red dot on the forehead which marked her as a married woman.

From all these restrictions imposed on my mother, I realized how much being stared at had bothered my dad.

New rules were also in place for my brother and me: we were to speak in English to my mother, to help her learn the language. I had a hard time embracing this sudden change, but I complied. After all, I thought practicing English would help me with school. My dad's oft-repeated motto for life in Canada was, "When in Rome, do as the Romans do!"

Thou wilt shew me *the path of life*: in thy presence is fulness of joy; at thy right hand there are pleasures for evermore. (Psalm 16:11, emphasis added)

Chapter 16

NEW SCHOOL IN OLD WINNIPEG

O my God, my soul is cast down
within me…
(Psalm 42:6)

Life was lonely. I had no friends. I would come home from school
and have no one to talk to. My brother, often preoccupied
with schoolwork or his toys, didn't pay much attention to me. My
mother never questioned me about my day at school nor took any
interest in me. My dad seemed distant and always busy.

The sparse scatterings of trees in front of our apartment seemed
to be the only life in the neighbourhood—if one could call it that.
Everyone kept to themselves.

We had no relatives in Canada except for my grandfather's
occasional visits from Kenya, or the one uncle, Bulus—my
mother's brother—who temporarily lived with us. I assumed he
had come to this barren land to escape my grandfather's abuses.

Much of my parents' conversations were spent with my uncle,
making plans for him to move to Toronto due to the lack of
space in the apartment, another large metropolis my grandfather
had also scouted.

Once one was available, we moved to an upstairs apartment,
which had a separate bedroom for my parents. My brother and I

each had a cot which at night could be unfolded and placed along opposing walls in the vestibule, with one end abutting the front door.

The kitchen had a gas stove, a medium-sized fridge, and a tiny table. From here, one could see a door with glass inlaid panels, which permitted a view of the balcony. But we were forbidden to go out on the balcony, as it seemed to be unstable, with many visible cracks in the base. The wood squeaked when we stood on it. The view wasn't much anyway—just the other two-storey rowhouses facing us from across the street.

I was always apprehensive about using the shared bathroom outside the apartment, across the hall, and up a few more stairs. This room had a large window with access to the roof. I often took a hurried shower and left quickly in case the man next door had to use the bathroom. We never saw him, but I would chant to myself to evade my fears.

I was bored in the apartment. I had one doll that we had brought from Kenya. My brother played with the battery-operated army tank given to him by my military uncle. The gun would fire and light up as it moved on the floor, to everyone's intrigue.

By accident one day, I realized that my red eraser from school could easily leave noticeable marks on the plaster walls. I began to rehearse my lessons aloud, marking the "blackboard" with the eraser. After each lesson, I would rub it off with my hand. This became my favourite pastime, and it worked to keep me engaged for hours. But what else was a seven-year-old to do? We weren't allowed to go outside to play, and I had no toys!

I was already struggling with my role as a female in a male-dominated culture and religion. Now, I had to admit to myself that this country viewed me as different in another way: as a dark Indian immigrant. Everyone in our community in Nairobi had been Indian. Students at school had been predominantly Indian as well. This was never an issue I ever had to deal with. I had never experienced racism so subtle and hurtful.

My new elementary school was a small two-storey red brick building. It was surrounded by asphalt with a high chain-link fence around its periphery. I felt like an outsider both inside and outside of the classroom, as it was not friendly and inviting. Somehow, the teacher informed my parents that I never participated in class nor talked to anyone. I *hated* school. I had no friends. Mrs. Adams wasn't the warmest teacher either.

My recess snack, a milk chocolate bar with a sky-blue wrapper bought from Dominion Store, was the only thing I looked forward to all morning, and my only delight all day long. Its rich creamy deliciousness, gently melting in my mouth, was like nothing I had tasted in Kenya. What a delight on those cold winter days.

My mother would walk my brother and me to school, but we often had to return home on our own. She would sometimes wait for us at a distance. It made me momentarily happy to see a familiar figure, but then my brother and I would walk in silence towards her, and walk home quietly the rest of the way.

I never enjoyed school. I never enjoyed the kids at school. I also never enjoyed life at home.

For when we were yet *without strength*, in due time Christ died for the ungodly. (Romans 5:6, emphasis added)

Chapter 17

FIRE!

…when thou walkest through the fire,
thou shalt not be burned; neither shall the
flame kindle upon thee. For I am
the LORD thy God…
(Isaiah 43:2–3, emphasis added)

One early October morning a short while after we had moved to Canada, we were awakened by my mother's frantic shouting: *"Fire!"* In panic mode, my dad hastily opened the door of the apartment for us to escape down the stairs. A puff of heavy black smoke billowed in, which made exiting through this doorway impossible. His next inclination, as we had rehearsed the night before after witnessing an apartment burning in the neighbourhood, during which a whole family died, was to grab our passport and document bag which was hanging behind his bedroom door.

My dad then instructed us to proceed swiftly in single file through the narrow kitchen to the dreaded, wobbly balcony that we were usually prohibited from standing on. Rushing past the gas stove on one side and the little dining table on the other, I glanced at my doll on a shelf, longing to grab it.

Outside, we stood shivering on the freezing concrete platform in our bare feet, with the bitterly cold autumn air penetrating our flimsy night clothing and into our bones.

Without hesitation, we began to yell in unison: *"FIRE! FIRE!,"* trying to rouse the neighbourhood and hoping someone would hear us. Not knowing the French word for *fire*, we made up for it by shouting. The noise got the attention of a couple living at the bottom level of the apartment across the street, who realized what was happening and called the fire department.

Neighbours also heard the commotion and ran over to the burning building to stand under the second-floor balcony, waiting to catch each of us as my dad handed us over the railing. When it was his turn, he climbed over the railing, slid down to the lowest rung, and jumped. His 5'11" height was an advantage, but his 250-pound weight caused an injury to one of his ankles.

The large, noisy fire engines soon arrived, with firefighters jumping out and pulling large hoses towards the building. With urgency and precision, they sprayed water into the old building, which had been built long before regulations about a sprinkler system or fire alarms!

We were told the fire had been started by a man smoking in bed in the apartment adjacent to ours. To escape, he had to jump out of his window, breaking his arm. Instead of alerting everyone in the building, he just ran away, to be later located by the police.

Still in our pyjamas and bare feet, the police escorted us into the police station. This was both humiliating and humbling. At that moment we realized that whatever little we owned was suddenly gone.

Two police officers took us to the Salvation Army depot, where we chose some used clothing. My proud parents found it difficult to accept charity, but had to put their feelings aside due to our desperate need to stay warm. Wearing worn-out second-hand clothes and shoes, the police drove us to a hotel room where we spent the night. Surprisingly, no one offered us food or money. I noticed my dad's distressed face as he tried to figure out how he was going to feed his family.

A day later, the authorities allowed my dad to re-enter the burnt apartment to retrieve some of our necessary belongings. My dad was hoping he could get an envelope containing cash from his last paycheque that he'd hidden in a drawer in his bedroom. He returned with the envelope and news that the apartment was drenched in water from the firehoses, and the stench of smoke was unbearable.

The money was divided into portions to pay for meals. We enjoyed some Coca-Cola and went outside, walking aimlessly down the street in front of the hotel. This allowed my burdened dad to figure out what to do in a place where we felt estranged, with no one to help us or give us any social assistance. Shortly after this stay, the police returned to take us to another apartment which had an adjoining common kitchen. I remember being hungry, but somehow we managed to buy some food with the remaining money. It was surreal not having a place to live while eating rationed food and wearing old clothes.

...God our Saviour; Who will have all men to be saved, and to come unto the knowledge of the truth. (1 Timothy 2:3–4)

Chapter 18

ROOM TO RENT

For thou wilt light my candle: *the LORD*
my God will enlighten my darkness.
(Psalm 18:28, emphasis added)

One day, my dad brought me along to the neighbourhood dry cleaner, where he had left a two-piece suit to be cleaned. That day, I overheard some bad news as he shared his predicament with the business owner: my dad had lost his job. The company he had been working for went bankrupt, and he was laid off without any pay. He also told the owner we'd had a fire in our apartment and now had no place to live and were being taken from place to place by the police. The kind owner offered the dry-cleaned clothing without charge, but my dad insisted that he would return with the money when he got a new job. The owner told us there was a woman he knew who had rooms to rent, and he would contact her.

A few doors down from the cleaners, we visited the woman with the room to rent. Madame Beaulieu was a plump, jovial, porcelain-white-skinned woman with a strong French accent. I instantly liked her friendly laughter and warm personality when she met us at the front door of her building.

As we entered the old, narrow, stale-smelling building, we were greeted by kittens of all colours scurrying freely throughout its two storeys. Various doors on one side of the front hall led to where other tenants lived.

We were escorted to the basement, where we saw a large room furnished with three neatly prepared beds already placed along the walls. A small window brought in some modest light, trying to brighten up the place. The adjoining room, which was once a storage closet, was now called "the kitchen." It contained a hot plate placed neatly on a table, which gave it the only right to that name. The large shared bathroom was the largest I had ever seen, with an old free-standing tub situated in the centre of the floor and an oblong window at the end overlooking the backyard.

We found out later that out of pity, the landlady had evacuated her own apartment to allow us to live there, while she moved into a large storage closet upstairs, transforming it into her bedroom.

The landlady was a pet lover. In addition to the cats and kittens, she owned a handsome black and white shepherd collie mix, Fido. This dog immediately sensed my fear, and would respectfully pass by me with its head hanging down and its tail between its legs in submission. In a short time, it won my confidence, and we became friends—at a distance.

Now that we had a place to stay, my dad asked permission from the fire department for a second time to try to salvage what he could from the apartment. We were escorted back to the burned building; this time, my brother and I accompanied my parents.

I remained outside waiting with Sohna, but looked curiously through the open front door. As my parents entered, cautiously climbing up the still-intact staircase, I gazed at the haunting view of the blackened main floor. At first, it looked too terrifying to follow them. Every time I attempted to step inside, I ended up running back out for fresh air. Sohna just stared solemnly ahead; I was surprised he was not inclined to explore, although I asked him several times to accompany me.

I was disappointed by how easily I was overcome by the nauseating air, which still smelled of smoke. The scent had even settled into the blackened walls and all the materials still left untouched by the fire. I remained outside. The entrance looked too eerie to re-enter. My brother still refused to come inside with me, so I patiently waited with him, overcome by the experience, hoping my doll would soon be rescued.

It seemed like a long time before my parents returned. They told us that everything was drenched with water from the firemen's hoses and had the reek of lingering smoke. They were not able to return with my doll, but retrieved my brother's army tank. I was told my doll was burned, but I did not believe them. They also brought back a set of prized *Children's Encyclopedia* books, still wet and smelling of smoke, which had been brought from Kenya. Everything else remained unclaimed in the apartment.

I did not understand the full impact the fire could have had on our lives. I was more concerned about getting back my doll, which I'd brought from Kenya, and the hurt I felt in losing it. What was important to the adults did not concern me. Sohna, four years older, recognized the danger we had been in, which affected him seriously. He began to get up every night, open the front door, and run into the middle of the street. His recurrent sleep-walking episodes continued for a long time, and particularly disturbed my parents. It was only then that I felt the reality of what could have been. After that realization, I did not care about the loss of my doll.

The new place was a little further away from the school we attended. I still hoped my mother would come to pick us up, especially after a time when, as I walked back alone from school, a chubby white girl with a devious smile decided to hit me for no reason I knew. With not much strength in my skinny arms to defend myself, I decided that at least I could run. I was surprised to notice that the *fat bully* was able to keep up with me. With the girl close at my heels, I entered a playground, running around the play structures a few times, only to turn around and see her flailing arms reaching out for me. I dodged them, frantically ran, and safely reached home, pleased she did not score a hit. After a few more attempts on her part to catch her prey, she finally lost interest and gave up, probably having to accept defeat. My running in my Kenyan days came in handy!

Kids in this country are not friendly, I thought. Many were not used to seeing children of my skin colour. There were a few black kids among the white majority, but I was still outnumbered here, being *brown.*

This was a hostile country which I did not like, for lots of reasons. The burned apartment held the last memories of Kenya. We were detached from the past, while a new life unfolded in this barren, chilly, and unfriendly country my parents called Canada. They talked about our new country with pride, but I did not agree.

We lived for a short time in old Winnipeg in the one-room basement apartment. The landlady was good to us until she began inviting my parents to attend séances with her. She claimed my dad would get the answers to his questions about the future from these meetings: he could receive messages by inviting the spirits of the dead. Something about these sessions was troubling and frightening to me. I was upset, and pleaded with my parents not to go. Despite my disapproval, my parents attended once a month, and then reported back on their experiences when they got home late at night. It was disturbing to hear about the instruments that started playing on their own and how my parents were able to talk to different spirits from their past through the help of their "séance leader."

The landlady preferred my brother over me, knowing I told my parents not go to these séances, so she informed my parents that I was very *different!* As a result, my dad shared with her the reason for my brother's favoured position, being a reincarnated priest, and how my dad was convinced that the priest was very tidy, just like my brother. To my father, that was the defining feature that proved it was him. I still didn't believe it for a moment. *I* was the one who was neat and tidy and a real organizer, but I was not that priest—nor was my brother!

I did not need any comments from anyone that would further distance my parents from me. I saw Madame Beaulieu as devious and cunning, and I no longer liked being with her. Behind her house was the abandoned shed where she stored what I would call junk. She gave us a tour of the place, then told us that *ghosts* lived there! When my parents were gone with her, my brother and I made sure Fido stayed with us as we were too afraid to venture into the backyard.

It was not long until my dad got a job at a bank's head office in downtown Winnipeg, shortly after our crisis; he soon became a manager working night shifts. We were able to move to a small two-bedroom apartment in a residential part of Winnipeg.

I was glad when I heard we would be moving to an apartment, but then I thought of my buddy, Fido. His furry jet-black body and white mane were stunning. Thunder frightened him, making him slide under the bed, but the rest of the time he was loyal and friendly, acting like a guard dog as he escorted us to the backyard. We enjoyed watching him drool as we ate green apples in front of him, then treated him to the fruit when no one was watching. When my brother and I were play-fighting, Fido would get in the middle and try to stop us, thinking we were hurting each other. On one occasion we even got silver paint on his side, when we were asked to paint the fire escape. The landlady was upset.

Fido was good-natured, even though my mother yelled at him for getting into the garbage. He stayed clear of her for weeks. I was going to miss my *only* joy at this place. Later, the old boy got cancer and had to be put down.

I am come a light into the world, that whosoever believeth on me should not abide in darkness. (John 12:46, emphasis added)

Chapter 19

OUR APARTMENT

…a man's life consisteth not
in the *abundance of the things*
which he possesseth.
(Luke 12:15, emphasis added)

Two years after we arrived in Canada, we moved to another residential suburb in Winnipeg. Most of the homes were duplexes and small army bungalows. Ours was the only rental apartment building in the area. It was surrounded by a bright aqua-green picket fence that was noticeable blocks away. Our modest apartment was just a few steps from the main entrance. The two bedrooms were small. My parents' bedroom was separated from the living room by a semi-sheer curtain. The other bedroom was narrow and was to be shared with my brother once we got some furniture. It had a long window looking out at a small bungalow across the street.

Down the hallway was a small closet for the clothes belonging to my brother and me. The bathroom at the other end of a long corridor was across from the kitchen, which had the essential appliances of fridge, stove, and a small dining table and chairs. The large window overlooked the backyard.

At first, my brother and I slept facing opposite directions on a couch in the living room that opened flat into a bed. A bedsheet covered the rock-hard teal textured upholstery fabric. When my parents had enough money, they bought us a bunk bed. Even though the furniture store owner tried to insist that my parents buy a ladder and side guard railing, they refused. I was to sleep on the top bunk and was expected to climb up by stepping on the frame of my brother's lower bunk. In theory it worked, except when my brother and I had a disagreement, which was often. Dodging his attacks on my delicate toes, it was critical that I get to my bunk as quickly as possible, unbeknownst to my parents. I was not to place my foot on his mattress, but hike up the side of the wooden frame. Even here I would get attacked with his fists.

On several occasions, I would roll off the top bunk, landing on the hard wooden floor to awaken with a loud *thud*. This never seemed to alarm the rest of the family very much. Somehow, I always managed to avoid hitting my head or sustaining any broken bones.

On one side of our bedroom was a narrow pressed-wood desk my brother used for his homework, while I worked on the kitchen table. Once his was replaced by a wooden one, three times the size, I inherited his old desk. My dad pointed out that my brother's possessions, including his clock radio, were worth three times mine. I remained silent, but was troubled that this information needed to be shared with me.

My desk had an interesting squeak as I pushed it back and forth, loosening the hinges, which I did when I was bored or upset. The attached cabinet at the front on one side had a sliding cardboard panel protecting a little storage space for me to keep some belongings: stationery, school projects, artwork, and letters my aunts Reena and Alka sent me from England and Kenya, respectively.

While I was at school, this personal space was frequently emptied of my special possessions and decluttered by my mother to ensure no junk accumulated in my desk. Her sifting through my treasures to get rid of them was annoying. I felt she did not trust me, and had to scrutinize the valuables I had hidden away.

I again learned to detach from anything I owned, so I would not miss it when it was gone. On the other hand, my brother never got his desk cleared out and never complained of missing items.

On the top shelf of our shared hallway closet was stored a porcelain mini tea-set that had once been given to me for an occasion. I rarely got to play with it, as it was a nuisance for anyone to hand it to me. *It will make a mess in the bedroom,* my mother would tell me. I wanted to pull up a chair and take it down, but worried it would be seen as an act of defiance if I helped myself to my own toys. Sometimes I would plead with my parents to bring it down so I could play with it, but it would soon end up back in its storage space.

My only doll, dressed in a pink flannel coat and very much like the one I had lost in the fire, was given to me one Christmas after I was very sick from the Hong Kong flu that passed through Canada in the sixties. I was too ill to appreciate the doll, so it remained behind glass in a bookshelf in the living room, for rare handling only.

At one Christmas gift exchange at school, someone gave me a flat cardboard doll including a wardrobe of cut-out paper clothes. I guarded this favourite toy in my desk, trying to make sure nobody would see me playing with it for fear it would be taken away, too.

My brother kept his army tank in the same glass bookcase, which he could take out and play with as he wished. Having survived the fire, it would still travel across the floor with its distinctive firing noise. Its movement across the floor, the shooting gunfire sound, and the light flicking on and off as it fired still entertained all of us.

My brother spent most of his free time playing Meccano. I was amazed at his ingenuity in being able to spend hours on Saturdays assembling a moving crane, complete with twine and moving parts. He would store his toys under his lower bunk.

On some occasions, my brother would make a stove or fridge out of the metal Meccano pieces. I could play with it for a short time until he needed to dismantle it for his own projects. At these sporadic times, we played together. Once, we asked for a puzzle we saw in a department store. We were each given a five-hundred-piece landscape puzzle, which we put together and pulled apart countless times, racing against each other.

Although we did not celebrate Christmas, we somehow persuaded our parents to get a tree. We owned the cheapest, skimpiest, most pathetic-looking tree, for which we fashioned paper decorations we had learned how to make at school. Our gifts to each other were used Bic ballpoint pens, which we had fun unwrapping on Christmas Day. This way we could tell everyone in school that we celebrated Christmas and opened gifts!

Most of our time in the apartment was spent on schoolwork. I would spend hours making intricate pencil or pastel drawings for school projects, memorizing multiplication tables, spelling words, or French grammar, and practicing cursive writing. Crafts like crocheting and knitting were not considered essential for school, so it was hard to convince my parents to get the necessary supplies due to their tight budget.

To keep me focused on school, other skills like washing dishes and cooking were ignored. I was not allowed to bake the recipes I learned in Home Economics. I also could not practice embroidery, which I had learned in one of the classes. I was not allowed to practice the recorder, melodica, or bass recorder which

I was specially selected to play, as my parents got complaints from the janitor that I was making too much noise with my instruments and was disturbing other tenants. To practice for exams, I could only finger the instrument and pretend I was blowing into it.

My brother was allowed to join the Boy Scouts, while despite my repeated requests, my parents refused to let me join the Girl Guides. When I would watch him come home in his uniform and see his excitement over the new badges he had earned, I became envious that he was so highly favoured. I knew I would be able to earn badges, too—if given the same opportunity.

Every weekday afternoon at 5:00 p.m., I was to prepare my dad's work clothes and make his lunch for his night shift. I was taught to lay a water-soaked handkerchief on the pant leg before using a steam iron to smooth out the wrinkles. The odour of the steam from the combination of the wet handkerchief and the fabric of the pants was nauseating. Next, I would iron his shirts, which were encrusted with Ban deodorant at the armpits, which the repeated washing could not remove. This would set off a dreadful smoke. Fighting back a headache and coughing from the strong fumes of the hot iron, I would grudgingly complete the task before me. It was a nasty ritual that I dreaded every day, as I always felt sick after this hated chore.

Next, I was instructed to make my dad's sandwich—"mock chicken" and cracked wheat bread with mustard. I sometimes added an orange or an apple to the brown paper lunch bag. My dad would leave abruptly and return in the middle of the night when we were all asleep.

When we were not working on schoolwork, we were allowed restricted television shows. To watch the old RCA wooden-framed black and white TV, we had to sit on the floor on a sheet spread out over the fake prickly Persian rug. This sheet became a battlefield between my brother and me. An imaginary boundary line was drawn down the centre and I was not to cross over to his side, or a powerful fist would come crashing down, smashing any toes or fingers in its way. The fingers and toes always happened to be mine, and the fist was always my brother's.

I had memorized the TV Guide, and could choose to watch anything between 7 and 11 p.m. My favourite shows were Hogan's Heroes, Lucy, Bonanza, Get Smart, Jerry Lewis movies, and the Dick Van Dyke Show. We were not allowed to watch any late-night shows or movies. This was the only time I laughed or enjoyed any escape during home life.

Sometimes a game of Monopoly would end up in a fight between my brother and me, when I realized he had snuck a few extra five-hundred-dollar bills from the bank when I went to the washroom. It was always when I was winning, which was often. If my dad was home sleeping during the day from his night shift, his angry response to being woken up was to rip the game in half. It had to be replaced a few times until we were no longer allowed to buy another Monopoly game.

In our fights, we even took the law into our own hands, fighting silently for fear of waking our dad, but somehow, I was always overpowered by my older brother. As I called him a cheater and a liar, he would propel a swift, powerful fist into my bony upper back, knocking out residual air—a feeling I experienced too often. As I gasped for air, nearly passing out, I would counterattack by grabbing the culprit's arm to prevent another blow. As he tried to escape, my grip would get firmer—then it would always happen! As my brother's arm slipped away and as my grip got stronger, my fingernails would get in the way! To my shock, the trail of my nails traced along my brother's arm was evidence of my *wickedness*. He would wait for the moment to proudly display my assaults on him to my parents to get their sympathy. For days my brother would nurse the war wounds, flashing them at me and inevitably at my mother. Touching the object of her heart was too much for her. Her disgust for me grew stronger.

In private, I experienced deep remorse for hurting my brother. I hated myself for being so cruel and so rough. It was unintentional! I always asked myself how it possibly could have happened. My parents never understood, nor listened to my side of the story. What provoked me to act this way was self-defense, but to my parents, I was a *vicious wild animal* attacking their favoured son.

Conversations with my mother were brief, stern, and emotionless, usually flavoured with her anger and verbal abuse. She was always on edge about something—often at me. It seemed I could never please her, no matter what I did.

I hardly ever saw my dad because of his shift work. He never talked to us when we got home from school. The weekends were meant for him to catch up on his much-needed sleep, so we had to remain very quiet during the day. In the evenings on Saturdays and Sundays, his favourite activity was watching television while sitting on the sheet on the carpeted floor. He especially enjoyed wrestling.

When my mother got pregnant with my sister, I intuitively started doing small chores for her. Sometimes I overheard my parents talking amongst themselves about my little acts, but nothing was ever said to me.

My sister, Khushi, was born when I was twelve years old. Her crib was in my parent's room. She brought so much joy to my heart and to the rest of the family. Most of my parents' focus was on her: a baby needing so much attention. My dad adored her as their only child born in Canada. My mother, unfortunately, decided to go to work. I was appalled that she could leave her baby at home with my dad. Being on the night shift, my dad did his best to look after my sister during the day while trying at the same time to get his sleep.

Alone at night, I began to rehearse the day's events of neglect and bad treatment by my mother. These thoughts gnawed at me when I tried to get to sleep. I began to ask myself, *Why does my mother hate me so much?*

My sadness turned to crying at night—thinking about my grandmother and remembering the happy memories of her love for me was heartbreaking. My private struggles continued, totally unknown to the others. Soaking my pillow with tears, turning it over, and eventually falling asleep became my nightly ritual for those years of elementary school.

My parents did what they knew best under the circumstances of being in a foreign land, mingling with people and their unfamiliar customs. They taught us what they knew according to the customs, beliefs, and traditions they had grown up with in India. Home life followed the same teachings and cultural expectations they had been taught.

The image I had of my father was of a strict head of the household. He spent little time with us individually. Whenever we would have visitors, a different side of him would emerge: a captivating storyteller leaving the hearers spellbound till the end, as he used to do in Kenya.

My mother was forced to accept the boundaries of what females could and could not do. She remained loyal to her cultural upbringing, attempting to pass those restrictions on to her daughters.

Most of the animosity that I faced at home was from my mother. I tried hard to understand why she acted the way she did and why I was always the *scapegoat* against whom she could freely lash out—often for unknown reasons. Sometimes various statements would sneak out about her home life for all to hear; she would openly express her inner frustrations when she thought things were getting rough or something triggered a memory of her past.

Piecing statements together, I formulated a picture of her hard life—something she could not often talk about. Whatever it was that haunted her from the past, it left her stoic, bitter, and miserable, unappreciative of anything good, and unable to show affection. I sensed she felt hostility towards her parents, primarily her father. I knew she still despised the limitations imposed upon her: having to quit school to stay at home and tend to household duties, unlike her sisters.

I was the dishonourable object, the *female child* my mother would have preferred not to have, based on her personal feelings and perhaps what I represented to society. It was my brother she chose, so she put me aside as an undesirable girl. This dark veil of hatred and aggression for me prevented her from noticing my sympathy and sensitivity for her.

> Then said Jesus unto them… I am come that they might have *life*, and that they might have it *more abundantly*. (John 10:7, 10, emphasis added)

Chapter 20

ANOTHER NEW SCHOOL!

But where shall *wisdom* be found? and
where is the place of *understanding?*
(Job 28:12, emphasis added)

The elementary school I attended for grade four was about one block down the street from where we lived. It was a small, two-storey red brick building with a high chain link fence around the periphery of two split yards at either end of the school. At one end of the asphalt-covered play area reserved for the younger kids, we played popular games like tag, elastics, skipping, hopscotch, catch, soccer baseball, and dodgeball.

For the first time since our arrival in Canada, I finally made friends—of course, all girls. The only time I could talk to them was in the schoolyard during recesses. They all went to each other's houses, but I always felt uneasy about explaining why I was not allowed. Even though I was close to some of them, I refrained from discussing my cultural and religious beliefs and our strict family restrictions for fear of embarrassment, knowing they would not understand and might even make fun of me.

Any time we were together as a group of girls, the boys would come around to tease us, wanting to be chased. All the girls would give in and run around the yard after them. Since I was forbidden to talk to boys, I would ignore them, hoping they would leave me alone, even though I enjoyed their attention. I remained calm and avoided reacting when I was called names like Tarzan, Rhino, or Jungle Bunny—they thought I came from the jungles of Africa. I was especially afraid of them following me home.

Every Friday we had arts and crafts. My work was often brought up to the front of the class by the teacher to point out its originality and beauty, and then displayed at the back of the class or even in the school hallway in front of the office. I enjoyed receiving praise from all the students. However, when I brought the artwork home and gave it to my parents, I never received the acknowledgement and praise I craved from them; instead, my creation would strangely be gone the very next day.

Realizing that my mother threw out my artwork upset me. I had to learn to numb the hurt feelings each time and try to remember the compliments of my classmates and teachers, and the feelings of contentment and pleasure I'd received at that time. That was my reward; it satisfied my need to be noticed and accepted, which motivated me to work even harder to please them.

One notable day, I was called to the principal's office. As I sat in front of him, confused and anxious, he assured me it was because I was a *very special student*. Not many, he emphasized, got to sign his personal book. As I looked up behind his head, I noticed something strangely familiar that shocked me! On the wall was a piece of artwork, so beautiful, delicate, and ornate! It was a familiar name made into a mirror image and decorated with roses. It was my name: *Rajkumari*! Where did *he* get my artwork? I felt privileged to be in this man's office, the principal we all esteemed. My heart skipped as I realized he was honouring my work—and my *name*—by displaying it in his office. I signed his book without comment and left in a daze!

Before leaving the front desk, I asked the school secretary if I would be allowed to keep the artwork. I was now convinced it was valuable. She assured me that I could keep it. However, when I brought it home, once again it was overlooked. When I showed my projects to my parents and repeated the comments made to me by the teachers, or told them how I had received the highest mark in an exam, I faced indifference every time. I never felt appreciated or valued by them for anything I did. *Maybe they do not realize how hard school is,* I thought, *not having gone through the Canadian school system.*

My mother had brought some handmade artifacts, white cotton crocheted tablecloths and placemats, with her from Kenya. I would have liked to have learned her skills. All the finely detailed exquisite handiwork which everyone praised her for was given away one piece at a time to her work colleagues. Perhaps it reminded her of those early bitter years when she was forced to leave school. She hated anything handmade—even gifts I made for her. Even the things my teacher thought were the best in class were worthy only for the garbage in her eyes.

After forming several friendships with my classmates and playing with them during recess, I developed social confidence and became fond of school. With impeccable attendance and exemplary schoolwork, I earned the respect of the students, but more importantly, the teachers and each principal.

The staff liked me because of my serious and well-behaved nature. They were so confident I never caused trouble in class that I was often allowed to go home while the rest of the class had to stay after school for a detention. This worked out in my favour, anyway, as my parents would have been angry if I came home late from school.

Once, a substitute teacher held me back after school with the whole class, but the regular teacher soon corrected the situation by letting me go home. I was even mistakenly given "lines to write" for misbehaviour like the rest of the class, but the regular teacher just dismissed the penalty given to me. Some students got frustrated and upset at the favouritism I received and started calling me the "teacher's pet." I never challenged them, but privately relished receiving the special treatment.

The two diametrically opposed worlds I lived in were a private, dream-like school life where I enjoyed activities and had fun with friends, and a strict home regime in a hostile, loveless environment where all my life necessities of food, clothing, and shelter were provided. At home, I hungered and had a need for praise, consideration, and attention; nevertheless, I went unnoticed and overlooked. No one asked me how things were going at school or asked anything about the teachers or my friends.

It was in Mrs. Peachey's grade five class, when I was eleven years old, that for the first time I talked to the friend sitting beside me during class, but the teacher never scolded me like she would have everyone else. It was like she was watching me cautiously crawl out of my safe shell, and did not want to disturb the delicate operation for fear of my returning and never coming back out again. I was still her best student, so she seemed to pull back from telling me to stop talking in class or laughing at my friend's jokes. I needed the release of a little freedom, and she seemed to know that somehow. That was the only year during which I acted giddy in class—perhaps it had something to do with the hormonal changes brought by puberty. I settled down and was once again serious in class after that.

My parents never attended parent-teacher interviews. The only time the school saw my parents was for one school concert and for graduation from grade seven. I had to plead to get my parents to finally attend. They seemed self-conscious about being the only Indians among so many white people.

Socializing outside of school was forbidden. Phone calls to friends were limited. I was too ashamed to explain to my friends that I was not allowed to go out to play or to talk for long on the phone.

An uncanny feeling of sadness and loneliness crept upon me when I was at home. I began to question in private why my perfect reports, projects with commendations, and awards were never acknowledged. I never got in trouble at school like some of the kids. No one at home even realized how well I was liked at school by everyone.

My mother seemed determined to have my hair cut very short. Instead of being sent to the women's hair salon, I was forced to regularly go to a barbershop with my brother, or sometimes alone. My mother would send me back to the shop if it wasn't short enough. Even the barber would be uncomfortable and would ask me why I did not go to a salon instead of coming to him for a haircut, wondering why it had to be so short. Returning to school, the boys would laugh at me for looking like one of them.

At school, I could not see the blackboard clearly, but I dreaded getting glasses as so few wore them, so I never told my parents. I thought it would give the boys another reason to mock me, so I would just copy from the student next to me. One day, the teacher noticed and asked the school nurse to have my eyes checked. A note was sent home promptly to my parents for me to see an optometrist, as I needed glasses. I went with my dad and selected the most affordable pair: black-framed cat's eye glasses! I knew the kids would laugh at me, so when I put them on at school to read the board, I would cup my hand around one edge, so as not be seen. The boys sometimes happened to turn around and see me, and they would always laugh and inform the rest of the boys. From then on, I would only use the glasses if I could not copy off someone beside me.

Sex education was a difficult and uncomfortable topic to bring up with my parents. Permission forms were sent home that they had to sign, indicating whether I was allowed to attend or not. Not having the courage to talk to them, I would just place the papers on the kitchen table. Each year, I would be reprimanded for bringing *such* forms home, so I would have to explain that they had to be signed. Of course, I was forbidden to attend. During the sessions in class, I would be singled out from the rest of the students by the teacher and asked to go to another classroom. Awkwardly, I would walk out, with everyone staring at me as I left.

…he that is perfect in knowledge is with thee. (Job 36:4)

…Christ; In whom are hid all the treasures of wisdom and knowledge. (Colossians 2:2–3)

Chapter 21

RESTRICTED PLAY TIME

For the LORD heareth the poor, and
despiseth not his prisoners.
(Psalm 69:33)

O ne of my classmates, Karen, lived across the street, so she
frequently rang our doorbell, asking me to come out to play.
Her repeated requests made my parents feel uncomfortable, and
they would finally succumb and let me play outdoors. Careful
instructions were given for *one hour of play*, and if that curfew was
exceeded, the privilege would be taken away. Also, I had to remain
close to the apartment, and was not allowed to enter anyone's
house.

My friend and I had fun playing hopscotch, soccer baseball in
the laneway, or hide and seek with other kids in the neighbourhood. Even though I was warned plentifully, not owning a watch
and lost in my play, the hour soon became two, then three. Having lost track of time, upon returning home, I commonly faced
the ordeal of irate words and threats to be banned from going out
again. Somehow, I enjoyed the play time so much that putting up
with the angry words from exceeding the curfew was worth it.

As I was not allowed to bring anyone inside our apartment, my
friend and I decided to find a place on the floor under the stairwell

in the lower level of the building. She would bring over her Barbie dolls with their wardrobe of clothing—I was not supposed to play with them because of their adult figures. This continued for a short time until the janitor who lived on the same floor complained to my parents that it might be a disturbance to the other tenants, even though we never made any noise. To stay close for my parent's sake, we decided to play inside the fenced-in grass area around the apartment. Once again, the janitor complained to my parents— this time that we were playing on the grass! We had to stop putting up our little yellow tent we got for free from Kool-Aid points.

Karen and I decided to go to the park a block away where we played hide and seek with a group of kids. I noticed a stretch of grassy field, so smooth and green, on one end of the park, inviting me to *run*! Although I tried to coax some of the kids to join me, I was left alone to run several lengths till I was out of breath. The exhilarating, liberating feeling of the wind rushing past my face, the haze of objects disappearing from my peripheral vision, effortlessly projecting forwards, captivated me like it did when I was in Kenya. Sweating, out of breath, but satisfied with feelings I did not even know I had—longing for *freedom*!

Not permitted to stray too far from the apartment, not allowed in anyone's yard or home, not able to invite anyone to come into our apartment to play: with all these restrictions and limitations, eventually, Karen found someone else she now called her "best" friend. The doorbell no longer rang with someone inviting me to come out to play.

My dad had moved us to Canada to provide us with better education and opportunities that he had never received in his poor upbringing. As I got older, I began to realize the emphasis on success in education was a bargaining tool in preparation for marriage, especially for negotiating a dowry from the bride's family. Physical appearance, level of education, family status, and even time spent living in a foreign country would allow a more prestigious arranged marriage, contributing to the honour of the family name and the reputation of the parents. These were standards set by *society*. The importance placed on education prevented me from being allowed to developing any other skills, like cooking, baking, cleaning, or enjoying hobbies.

> The Spirit of the Lord is upon me [Jesus], because he hath anointed me to preach the gospel to the poor; he hath sent me to heal the brokenhearted, to preach deliverance to the captives, and recovering of sight to the blind, to set at liberty them that are bruised... (Luke 4:18)

Chapter 22
PRACTISING HINDUISM

Thou shalt not make unto thee any
graven image, or any likeness of any thing
that is in heaven above, or that is in the
earth beneath, or that is in the water
under the earth. Thou shalt not bow
down thyself to them, nor serve them:
for *I the Lord thy God am a jealous God...*
(Exodus 20:3–5, emphasis added)

The narrow bedroom my brother and I shared had a linen
closet at one end, in which my parents set up a shrine of idols
and pictures of Hindu gods and goddesses on the centre shelf.
Once a week my mother would make cotton wicks which were
dipped in homemade ghee and placed on a brass dish for burning.
This practice stopped when my father expressed his concern about
starting a house fire. Instead, my mother began to burn incense
sticks, which filled the apartment with their fragrance.

It was here that my parents insisted that I acknowledge the
shrine by chanting the names of Hindu gods, just as my brother
did regularly. I did not really want to stand in front of the open
closet to chant aimlessly, but I did—more out of curiosity

than obedience. To my child-like mind, instead of an uplifting experience, the framed pictures frightened and disturbed me.

My inquisitive eyes did not understand the menagerie of strange, surreal pictures of gods, goddesses, and colourful animal figures. The one time I stood staring and studying the images for a very long time, I was terrified to see a woman with many arms protruding out of her body, sitting on a large wild cat; a blue-coloured male carrying a bow and arrow with a wrapped snake around its neck; a seated part-elephant part-human with a flowing trunk; several female goddesses with exaggerated breasts; a flying monkey with the facial features of a man; and a healthy white cow adorned with a wreath of pretty flowers.

On some Saturday evenings, my dad would suddenly stop our play or schoolwork, and gather us to sit cross-legged on the floor in a circle on our tiny bedroom wooden floor. With the lights turned off, he would start the monotonous chanting of names of Hindu gods for us to follow. The goal, he emphasized, was to achieve a deep enough focus to eventually see a "light." This would indicate the presence of the gods, and our ultimate desire should be to become *one* with them. Although I cooperated, it seemed like a meaningless exercise and a waste of time. I tried but did not see any "light." I felt nothing spiritual from the boring repetitions, but never questioned my dad—so as not to offend him, but especially to prevent an outburst of anger.

On weekend mornings, my dad would come out of the shower with a huge bath-towel draped around his lower half, muttering the same chant I heard for years in his smooth, mellow deep voice. While the melodic singing tone was pleasant to the ear, I found the tiresome, unintelligible words annoying. During the week, it was in the late afternoon after his shower that he would perform his customary act, before getting ready for his night shift at the bank. I admired the consistency with which my dad performed this ritual.

One day, my brother announced to my parents that he was going to write out the names of Hindu gods repeatedly, to my parent's great delight. To me, it seemed as if he was writing out lines, like a punishment for school. *I can do that too,* I thought. Pages and pages of writing out the same word, or a chant sentence, while I was watching TV. I soon gave up, not feeling any benefit from this tedious exercise. It seemed insignificant to my child's mind, but I kept all these feelings of uncertainty and confusion to myself.

None of these experiences answered the questions which began to burden me about life: its meaning and purpose. One day, I decided to share my questions with my brother, Sohna: "Why are we here on the earth? What is the meaning and purpose of life? Who are we?"

My brother immediately broke out in laughter at my ridiculous questions and mimicked me, adding a satirical spin as he ran off to play. Self-conscious and embarrassed by his reaction, I never asked these questions to anyone again.

In my early years, I was confused and had many questions about life. My parents were trying to pass on what they were taught about Hinduism, which they had learned from their upbringing in India. I did not want to blame them or go against them, and had no intention of rebelling, but I found repetitively chanting the names of Hindu gods endlessly in a dark room *meaningless*; praying to pictures and statues seemed *futile*; and writing out words on a piece of paper also seemed *pointless*. I did not get any satisfaction or fulfillment from any of their religious activities. What my heart was searching, longing, and aching for was something *deeper* and more *profound*. I did not fully recognize my need at that time, but it left my heart and mind yearning for answers to my questions.

Then spake Jesus... *I am the light* of the world: he that
followeth me shall not walk in darkness, but shall have the
light of life. (John 8:12, emphasis added)

Chapter 23

EXPOSURE TO CHRISTIANITY

My beloved… shewing himself
through the lattice.
(Song of Solomon 2:9)

…for that which had not been told them
shall they see; and that which they had
not heard shall they consider.
(Isaiah 52:15)

The school I attended was Protestant, so each student received a small Gideon New Testament annually. Whenever I took mine home, before I had the opportunity to read it, it would oddly disappear; I would find out later that my mother routinely threw it out.

The first half hour of each morning was spent singing the national anthems, "O Canada" and "God Save the Queen," followed by songs out of our class hymnbook. I became familiar with hymns like "Jesus Loves Me," "When Mothers of Salem," "Work Beside the Father's Bench," and "All Things Bright and Beautiful." Students could raise their hands to select hymns; I never chose any, even though I liked the pretty tunes. That was all I knew about this Protestant religion—certainly nothing about the Jesus we would sing about.

In music class, we were taught hymns for school concerts at Easter and Christmas. I often practiced them out loud in the shower. My favourite hymn became "The Lord Is My Shepherd," written by Francis Rous, to the catchy tune of "The Happy Wanderer." I knew the hymn well, but did not know the Shepherd we were singing about.

> The Lord's my Shepherd, I shall not want.
> He makes me down to lie
> In pastures green; He leadeth me
> The quiet waters by.
> *Refrain:* He lives! He lives! He lives! I know that my
> Redeemer lives!
> He lives! He lives! He lives within my heart.

The class was asked to come to school early one morning to practice for an upcoming concert. The first hymn on the agenda was "The Lord Is My Shepherd." As I began to sing in the choir, suddenly I looked up from the sheet music, feeling the need to scan the whole room. All I saw was the music teacher playing at the piano; the rest of the front of the room was empty. However, I had an overwhelming awareness of the presence of *Someone* in the room I could not see! Startled, I continued to sing. I never shared the experience with anyone else.

For months following, I rehearsed that moment, revisiting the unique experience in my mind, wondering Who the *Unknown* and *Unseen Visitor* I had so deeply felt was! I was both confused and bewildered.

After the evening concert, a parent approached the music teacher and questioned who the little girl was who she saw "singing with all her heart." My music teacher shared this comment with me, which surprised me. I wasn't sure why the woman would have picked me out from the rest of the class, as I did not even know about *Whom* I was singing!

One eventful day, a girl brought a large, glossy book to school to show to the rest of the class. It was passed around from student to student, but when I got ahold of this book, the pictures and words captivated me. I had never seen anything like it. The colours were beautiful. There were no horrific pictures, no torture scenes, no darkness, no hatred, or violence… but it depicted a Man standing on the top of a hill talking to a crowd of people. His face appeared so gentle and calm… so lovely… so sweet. The description in the text called this Person *Jesus*. The caption under the picture read: "Jesus said, Love one another." The words struck a chord in my heart. I was mesmerized by the message!

The teacher announced an art contest with the theme "Love in the World." At first, I drew a picture of the earth with people from all nations around the periphery holding hands. I noticed some classmates starting to copy my work, so I decided to scrap it, wanting to come up with a new idea.

My mind kept returning to that intriguing book my friend had brought to school, so I asked the girl to bring it back for use for the art contest. I turned to the page which had fascinated me the most, the message this Jesus was telling the people: *"Love one another."* I was so absorbed and excited with the idea of love, and the instruction this Man gave to the people. It seemed the book contained a secret message I wanted to share! It was *love* I desperately needed and wanted in my life. *Love* was the one thing I was seeking for and lacked in my home and my personal life. I felt a renewed sense of exhilaration and enthusiasm!

My pastel work on a white Bristol board was colourful, and a good likeness of the picture I was reproducing: a Man standing on a hill, teaching the people. I wrote this important, heart-wrenching message in cursive black ink in the space below: *"Jesus said, Love One Another."*

The classmates surrounded me and admired the artwork. When my teacher came by to look at it, she too commented positively, but then I overheard her remark as she turned to another teacher who had also come by to look at my work: "It is too bad that she will not win!" She added that the contest was sponsored by a Jewish synagogue, which would display all the artwork! I did not understand why that was significant, and why she had already suggested that I would not win. I was shattered.

The school librarian was fond of me. I was the kind of serious, hardworking student she was looking for to help her with her load of work. My job was to put books away neatly on the shelves, stamp them out for the students during library time, and reliably come in during lunch to clean up the library. I was given special permission to work alone, and took the privilege seriously, picking up the key from the office.

One lunch afternoon, a few classmates not so serious about working decided to accompany me, supposedly to help me complete the library work. However, once the door was shut and locked, they decided to play tag. This included running on top of the pristine oak tables. In the excitement of the play, I joined in as we ran, but were not aware of the noise we were making. The ruckus soon attracted the attention of the principal, who also trusted me, and was puzzled by the noise coming out of the room. When he knocked, there was complete silence before I opened the door, assuring him we were not running around as he had heard. I feared losing my job. He remarked if that kind of clamour would continue in the future, I would no longer be allowed to work in the library alone, and certainly not bring my friends. I had never been scolded by any school staff before, but tried to protect my friends, who were hiding in the closet. All future lunch work was done in the presence of the librarian, who had to have her lunch in the room.

Although I had allowed students into the library without her permission, the librarian permitted me to continue. At the end of the year, it was my job to wash the plastic covers of the books with soap and water or replace them if they were too damaged. She would even fight my distraught class teachers to allow me time to help her. The teachers insisted they needed me in class, and that I should not be her "labour force" in the library. Ultimately, the librarian won, and I carried on my chores faithfully to satisfy her high standards.

I was a good listener and readily followed her instructions. In turn, she would bake delicious chocolate brownies for my birthdays and the end of each school year. One year she gave me a gold Pisces charm. It was the only piece of jewelry I owned which my mother decided to keep. I was also pleased to receive a big old Children's Bible Storybook which she rescued from the discard pile in the library at the end of the school year. Taking it home one evening, I began to read from the first few pages to my brother, but it mysteriously disappeared before I got too far. I did not understand what I had been reading, anyway.

> ...these are written, that ye might believe that *Jesus is the Christ, the Son of God;* and that believing ye might have life through his name. (John 20:31, emphasis added)

Chapter 24

SICKNESS

A bruised reed shall he not break, and
smoking flax shall he not quench, till
he send forth judgment unto victory.
(Matthew 12:20)

Although my home environment was becoming increasingly unbearable and unpleasant, instead of feeling hostility and animosity towards the family, I had to learn to believe that I *deserved* this system of inequality between males and females. I struggled with accepting that I really did not merit what my brother received in favours. I had to admit to myself that I was too deficient and inadequate to ever measure up to my parents' standards or please them. As my self-esteem and self-worth plummeted, deep down I felt *shamed* and *unwanted*.

Sometimes, watching my brother indulging in more ice cream and Coke, or receiving bigger gifts and freedoms, gave me courage to point out the disparities to my mother. This only provoked her to get back at me with crude remarks that I was very jealous. I never found out where she had learned that dreaded word, "jealous," which was now included in her limited English vocabulary. A new array of words began to be freely hurled at me with disdain and emphasis: *"jealous-pitty,"* meaning one who is jealous. Another common name for me was *"pook-key,"* for someone in a lowly state of hunger and deprivation. I was also called *"ser-mooney,"* one who is dishonoured by having their hair cut short. This felt particularly unfair as I was forced to have my hair cut short—it was never my choice. Another word used for me was *"paa-ghal,"* a name for someone who is stupid.

Words I had heard my mother use to refer to me in tones of disgust and anger in Kenya were never used in connection to my brother, so I learned they were negative. Now, I was old enough to understand the meanings of some of these terms.

I often felt cornered and unable to defend myself, not knowing why I was being lashed out at. *It must be true,* I would think, *there must be something wrong with me!* Nothing I did was good enough for praise. As time went on, my anxious and depressed feelings haunted me and deprived me of rest as I lay in bed, while everyone else was asleep. Sometimes in the middle of the night, I would wake up with intense nausea and a sudden urge to throw up my supper. This need became more frequent.

Why could I not jump down from the second level bunk and madly dash down the hall to the bathroom, instead of inevitably depositing the ghastly mess on the carpet—the *new* carpet? Why couldn't I have warning signs? Why did I have to wake the family by making my retching sounds, only to be scolded for ruining *another* new carpet?

Somehow, I always seemed to know subconsciously when a new carpet was laid down, and as hard as I tried, I always left my mark. When the carpet had to be thrown away, I felt guilt-ridden. The harder I tried not to be a delinquent, the more likely I would get sick again—and on the *area carpet*, of course, and especially if it was new! It was like a stubborn tongue playfully invading the empty space of a missing tooth—it was only natural my vomit would gravitate towards the new carpets!

My mother scolded me, to no end. I was lectured not to compete with my brother in how much I ate, not to eat as much ice cream as he did; even the Coke I drank was supposed to be substantially less than his portion. I was jealous of what my brother ate, she scolded, and I must eat less. That was her explanation for why I would get sick.

My brother made fun of me by reproducing the audible sounds of vomiting. From then on, the team of my mother and brother unsympathetically referred to my vomiting by these same sounds. "No excessive food for you, or you will *'broughgh-broughgh'* at night," stated my mother, with my brother laughing in the background.

No one asked me how I was feeling or why I had the urge to throw up. I would not have been able to explain, anyway. I thought it was normal. But somehow the carpet, new or old, held more value than *me*.

Something about this situation made no sense to me: I never overindulged. Most of the time I hardly had an appetite to eat, and picked at my food. At school, my growling stomach would frequently get my attention, reminding me that I was hungry; I always hoped no one could hear it.

Why did kids make fun of me for being so "skinny" if I ate so much, like my mother said? There was only one girl skinnier than me, but she had porcelain white skin, big saucer green eyes, and wore nice clothes, which made up for her thinness. She was the last to be picked for teams in a sports game. I was the second to last, even though everyone knew I could run fast.

As if the throwing up was not bad enough, I would wet the bed well into age nine. I dreaded and feared urine from the mattress dripping onto my brother on the bunk below on those mornings. The thought would disturb me. Nothing should fall on my *sacred* older brother, and especially not urine. Although the thin bunk mattress would get surprisingly saturated, watermarked with the memories of the many "accidents," it never allowed a drip!

Nobody came to my rescue in the night, even if I called. Too tired to get up, I would stay in bed in wet clothing and wet bed sheets and fall asleep till the morning. Reeking of stale urine, wet pyjama bottoms stuck to my legs, I would wake up feeling the humiliation and embarrassment of my body performing independently of my will. My mother would reprimand me for the rancid smell and the work required to change the sheets on my bed as I got ready for school. *It must be a part of growing up,* I thought, *this bed wetting.*

My dad, working night shifts at the bank, did not *seem* to be aware of my mother's verbal abuse, unkind treatment, and lack of care towards me. On returning home in the middle of the night, he would sometimes hear me moaning from a stomach-ache and ask my mother to check up on me. Despite my dad's prompting, I would be left alone for hours, tossing and turning from abdominal pain. Mustering up enough energy, I would eventually make my way to the medicine cabinet in the bathroom to help myself to *any* medicine: Phillips Milk of Magnesia in a cobalt blue opaque bottle or aspirin tablets often came to my rescue. In desperation, I took whatever dose I thought I needed, swallowing it in the bathroom, and drinking the water from the tap.

One day, my dad sponsored my cousin, Bowen. His plea was accepted by the immigration department, and my cousin arrived from India. The problem was that there was nowhere in the apartment for him to sleep. It was decided between my parents and brother that the only solution was to give the top bunk bed to my brother and the lower one to my cousin. I thought I would get the teal upholstered couch that my parents had unfolded for my brother and me to sleep on when we were waiting for our bunk beds to arrive. But again, I overheard the family, especially my older brother, arguing that I would ruin the couch. Everyone agreed. The verdict was in: I must sleep on the wooden living-room floor, carpeted with the thin area rug. "She should sleep on the edge of the carpet," my brother remarked to my mother, "so she doesn't *ruin* it." To my surprise, even the hard teal couch and carpet rated higher than me.

My dad insisted I sleep close to the floor vent to stay warm, not realizing that breathing the furnace's dry, un-humidified air for the next two years would wreak havoc on my breathing. Without warning, I developed a new condition: uncontrollable coughing fits, shortness of breath, and heaving. The only way I figured out to catch my breath was to run to the bathroom and breath in steam from running hot water each time I got an attack.

One day out of curiosity, I decided to look up at the mirror *while* I was panting, wondering why everyone else looked on with frightened looks as I struggled for air. I was terrified to see a miserable beet-red face gasping for air. Watery eyes, strained neck and face muscles, and strange anxious sounds coming out of a distressed face. I was scared, and it was *me!*

My cousin, Bowen, who felt it was a serious situation as he watched me writhing for air, insisted my dad take me to a doctor. The incompetent old doctor had no explanation or treatment for what my dad tried to describe; when he tried to pronounce the word "asthma," he said *"esth-the-ma"* with his strong Punjabi accent. I tried pronouncing the word for my dad, but the impatient doctor, frustrated with my dad's explanation, just excused us and we went home.

One day, after running laps in the humid gymnasium at school, I experienced the same asthmatic attack I had at home, but even more severe after exercise. Everyone in the class stopped running, stood, and watched as I gasped noisily for air. Once I got my breathing back to normal after several minutes, my gym teacher announced: "You are never to run again!"

I could *not* end the activity I loved. I had loved it in Kenya. I loved it in Canada. It gave me the elation of freedom that I longed for. I was sad that this activity was taken away from me.

One evening, my mother asked me to get bread and milk from the grocery store, even though she could hear my rough, erratic coughing. Telling her that I was sick made no difference. As my brother sat in good health watching television, my mother continued to insist I go shop for the groceries. "Why can't Sohna go?" I pleaded. The more resistance I showed, the more pressure my mother applied to force me to go. I was confused and shocked that her treatment of me had come this far!

I started by refusing to go because I was sick. It became a battle, and finally my mother warned me she would strike me with her slipper. I provoked her to go ahead. She won—she hit me! I had never spoken back to my mother, but when she struck me that day, I felt her *hatred* for me had reached an epitome. Like a hurt, helpless animal, I yelled out with all the pent-up feelings of insecurity, all the load of injustices, all the feelings of neglect, all the verbal abuse and lack of love I had received: "I hate you! I hate you! I hate you!" It upset and shocked me to hear these ugly words coming out of my mouth.

I got my socks and shoes on, sobbing quietly as I stepped outside into the gloomy evening. As I tried to contain the blend of asthmatic coughing and crying, I projected a sound like an amateur symphony without an audience. Trying to understand my mother's bias, trying to make sense of what happened, I held back tears as I entered the store.

I walked back home alone in silence. I did not try to have a conversation with myself about the incident. There was irreparable damage in my heart, and I knew that comforting words to myself would not take away the pain.

I laid the needed essentials on the table. Alone, with a broken heart full of sorrow that no one cared about, I entered my room.

My brother taunted me by repeating the same words that had come out of my hasty mouth countless times in the following weeks. As salt is poured into an open wound, his words bit me afresh. It was his way of reminding my mother of my *evil nature*.

It was the first time in my life that I truly recognized that something was wrong with this picture. I never apologized to my mother, as I did not know how. I did not have the words, but deep inside my heart, not only did I suffer the emotional pain of how I was being treated, but now I had to live with the deep sorrow and guilt of yelling at my mother and telling her that I hated her. I did not hate her—I knew I did not. I have never hated anyone, ever.

That night, I wrote a private letter to my dad and put it in the mail pouch in his closet to tell him what had happened. When he got home from his night shift, he read it. But hearing my mother's version of the event, my dad did not question me. The outcome was settled: I was disobedient and had refused to get some groceries for her. The case was closed, never to be brought up again.

When Bowen moved away, I re-claimed the top bunk and no longer had to sleep near the heating vent on the floor. Although the severity of my breathing problem diminished significantly, and my overall condition improved dramatically, the residual weakness in my respiratory system always remained, making me prone to bronchitis and a milder version of asthma. Even after the teacher's scolding, I still ran outside in the park near the apartment when my brother and mother walked over there some evenings.

When I was eleven, episodes of cramps in my abdomen caused me to curl up in a fetal position and twist and wind for hours on the cold ceramic bathroom floor, trying to get comfortable. For fear of vomiting, I would remain in the bathroom, scanning the medicine cabinet to grab whatever I thought would relieve that pain. Once again, Milk of Magnesia came to the rescue. I tried to dampen my cries, but sometimes I would get the attention of my mother, who insisted that I open the door. I would feel ashamed as she watched me lie there, just helplessly staring. She would leave, mutter something to my dad, and return, but she offered me no help. I assumed it was just another part of growing up.

One terrible day, I was devastated to see blood on my underclothing. I thought I was bleeding to death and was going to die! My mother reproached me for leaving blood-stained clothes on the floor for all to see. But I *wanted* everyone to see what was happening to me—I was ill!

She offered me some sanitary products without any explanations, but told me to record the date of these episodes. Whatever did that mean? Somehow my friends must have seen stains on my clothing and told me in private it was called a "period" and it was a normal monthly cycle. For most of them, menstruation started at fifteen years of age; I was eleven.

My dad made an appointment for me to see the family doctor to get an explanation for these cramps. I was to go at the end of the school day, and happened to be the last patient of the day. The doctor told the receptionist to leave, then came back to tell me to undress completely and sit on the examining bench. There I sat as the *creepy* doctor surveyed my nude body with his peering eyes, told me to get dressed, and offered me sleeping pills to get better rest. I left, never to return, and my parents never asked me what the doctor had said about my pain.

Not being allowed to attend sex education classes, and spending little time with friends, I still did not understand what was happening to my body. Having never been given the opportunity at school or home to learn about puberty, I remained confused. I started becoming a woman at such an early age, but I did not feel like one. I felt like a scared child trapped in a woman's body. Noticeably developing, I tried to accept the changes, but I was told by my mother that I must conceal my body's new shape with layers of clothing. *It must be dishonourable to be a woman,* I thought, *and the forces of nature are making a mistake.* It was bad enough that I was not valued as a female; to try to change my identity and make me feel shame about my body, which I had no control over, made me feel insignificant and valueless.

My mother told me all my teeth would fall out if I didn't brush them, but as she didn't tell me how to do so correctly, I began to brush horizontally. I always seemed to have cavities from my poor diet and dental hygiene. I ate sugary cereal with white toast and jam for breakfast. At lunchtime, I would come home and eat white bread and jam again. Evening snack was a piece of white bread soaked in milk and sugar. The evening meal was a vegetable dish served with white bread and sometimes sour cream.

My dad did not have much of a dental plan, so visits to the dentist were only for emergencies. I only went after complaints about ongoing pain in my teeth. The only time any molars were removed were when they were so badly rotten with black cavities that only the four white corners protruded out, like the towers of the Taj Mahal.

My life at home consisted of schoolwork. I no longer cared for television. My friends had found other friends who could spend time with them, and I was alone.

In my private struggles—my struggles to belong, to be noticed, and to be valued—the forefront message was the lack of family *love* for me. It was a world of misunderstandings, inequalities, and biases—prejudices that I faced for being a female, something which I had to accept but also wanted to escape, desperately.

I continued to try to understand my mother's behaviour. Even though I did not know *all* the reasons my mother acted the way she did towards me, I concluded perhaps it was an effect of the injustices she must have faced growing up, losing all liberties, and being displaced in her position as a woman. What made her so stoic, bitter, cruel, and unable to show love and care for others, but especially *me?* I saw a hurt woman carrying hatred, animosity, jealousy, resentment, and bitterness inside of her, allowing these feelings to destroy the quality of her life. Her badge of self-pity persisted, and made others around her miserable, too. Every wound she must have experienced in her life remained etched deeply into her harsh face and heart, making her self-centred and selfish.

As time went on, I watched my mother's behaviour towards others. She was angry with the world and anyone who would wrong her. Anyone who my mother felt got out of line faced her *wrath,* primarily in the form of bitter gossip, proving their unworthiness to be her acquaintance, and reprimanding her family to have the culprit annihilated from any relationship. Any sign of unfaithfulness towards her received her condemnation for life. She never reconciled with anyone who would cross her. She never forgave. She never moved on. The accounts of every human she was in contact with were always laid out bare before her, and she made sure everyone knew how that person had wronged her, *repeatedly*. One person added to another, and then another, and yet another, as the list got longer. She was alone in her suffering, and all who knew her were uncomfortable around her. She trusted no one. Sometimes she would befriend an old enemy but only to again cross-examine them if they failed her.

I was trying to understand what made my mother's behaviour so aggressive and unfriendly, besides her upbringing. Would I ever understand my mother's bitterness with everyone and her suspicion that everyone was acting against her? But more importantly, why did my mother *hate me* so much?

It was the culture, values, and beliefs dictated by society and religion which made my parents react and form decisions and behaviours regarding where I stood in the hierarchy at home and where my place was in reference to my brother. Once again, my dad was convinced he must provide and give the best of care to my brother, who he thought was a deceased guru friend who had saved his life in India, now reincarnated as his son. My mother remained encapsulated by bitterness and pain from being displaced in the hierarchy in her own upbringing and needing to give up so many things, instead of breaking the cycle of biases. She just fell into the same pattern, becoming a woman who favoured and valued her son over her daughter.

> Why art thou cast down, O my soul? and why art thou disquieted within me? *hope thou in God;* for I shall yet praise him, *who is the health of my countenance, and my God.* (Psalm 42:11, emphasis added)

Chapter 25

FRIENDLESS

My heart panteth, my strength faileth me:
as for the light of mine eyes,
it also is gone from me.
(Psalm 38:10)

At the end of the school year, the teachers announced a sewing project for the girls: we were to learn to sew our own dresses. They would provide the necessary instruction and the use of sewing machines, but the parents had to buy the materials and the sewing patterns. My parents, needing to budget, did not want to waste money on crafts, so asking them for fabric and accessories was a challenge. When I explained that it *was* a school project, they finally allowed me to buy some cheap thin orange cotton fabric with a little pink and white flower print. My project was a simple long dress, so I added a pink sash at the elastic waist.

Our school uniform was a navy tunic with a white blouse, but to our surprise, we were told that we were to wear the dresses we had made to the evening graduation ceremony! Even though they had never attended any of my school concerts or teacher interviews, surprisingly my parents agreed to attend the ceremony after I asked them multiple times.

When my name was called, I walked awkwardly onto the stage, trying not to fall as the flimsy dress clung to my legs. I had never wanted to be seen in public with this dress, and especially not on the stage to receive my graduation certificate. My parents left immediately after the event without conversing with anyone. I wondered if they felt outnumbered because of their skin colour once again. I was unable to keep up with them as they rushed home. The subject was never brought up again. My mother's opinion of the dress must have been like mine—it mysteriously disappeared the next day.

Now that we were all promoted to grade eight, the students split up to different schools. What a difference that summer made! I lost touch with many of the old friends I knew from elementary school over the summer holidays, as I was no longer part of their social circle.

The transition school for grade eight included students from a whole new district. One lunch break, I happened to find a group of my previous classmates with whom I had never been very close. No matter how friendly I was in listening to their problems or making sure I met up with them each lunchtime for a walk, they seemed to remain in their cliques, and I was just a tag-along. We would put our lunch money together to buy huge chunks of chocolate from the candy shop to divide amongst us. Sometimes we would buy hamburgers from a popular fast-food restaurant near school. As my friends would discuss movies or music groups which I knew nothing about, I remained quiet, listening and trying not to reveal my ignorance. Who was Neil Diamond anyway? I had never heard the music of Alice Cooper, but from seeing pictures of him, I did not like his sinister look or the snake wrapped around his neck!

It soon became obvious that I did not fit in. Their interests in musical groups and artists and movies were foreign to me. Eventually, it seemed futile to make the daily effort to be with my friends only to be rejected. When I stopped meeting up with this group, no one asked me where I was or told me that they missed seeing me. No one seemed to look out for me either. They just did not want me around. Trying to force friendship was only getting me disappointed and hurt.

Listening to conversations in class, it was apparent that some of the students were taking drugs and following a promiscuous lifestyle with several partners. Drinking, smoking, and partying were prevalent. Hearing of sexually transmitted diseases amongst the students was not uncommon.

The school culture had a hierarchy. The more popular kids were at the top of the rank: wearing the best clothes, having the best teeth and hair, and being admired and talked about by everyone. They were like rock stars with a following, but were not necessarily the best students.

Making new friends was difficult. Those with whom the students mingled at school were the ones they partied with outside of school. As I was still not allowed to socialize with anyone, this left me friendless and alone. Besides, I looked like somewhat of an oddity, not wearing the latest fashion trends the popular kids wore. I could not even compete with the poorer students who maintained the trends. I began to feel the oppression, the loneliness, the isolation from other students. The esteem and praise I was longing for from students were no longer there.

Teachers in high school did not know students personally as they did in elementary school. I was one of many students, lost in the crowd. We had several teachers now, but for the most part no one favoured me or separated me out from the rest like I had been used to. My geography and science teachers were intrigued by the work I handed in, but they remained distant.

Although my eighth grade was a lonely year, I still focused on schoolwork. I still managed to achieve remarkable grades and a report card full of accolades. Each research project was typed with an aqua-coloured Brother typewriter, so old that the fading ink ribbon spool fed into it could no longer be replaced. I still accompanied each project with pencil or pastel drawings, so some teachers could ascertain my artistic talent by looking at my assignments.

In particular, my science teacher seemed to be impressed when he saw my "heart" project. I had typed over a hundred pages and included many colourful pastel drawings of blood vessels and the parts of the heart, copied from a medical textbook. Along with my "perfect" mark, on a separate lined paper he had written a note in red ink which said, "You can be anything you want if you choose to do so…" I read those words incessantly, trying to contemplate in my head what he meant. Could he see some value in me and even a future purpose which others could not—myself included?

Time and time again, I would pull out the letter, which was safely hidden in my project, tucked away in the back of the cardboard particle-board desk. Each time, I would try to decipher the message written in red. Reading it did give me some comfort and elation at the time, but it would also leave me confused. Ultimately, despite the letter, my identity, my self-esteem, and my self-worth continued to spiral downwards. I began to lose a sense of my own significance and any desire to live.

One day, as I passed by the side bedroom window of our apartment walking home from school, I noticed a boy not far behind me—someone whom I had seen in one of my classes and often on this street, also heading home. He quietly greeted me as he passed by, which I courteously acknowledged with a nod. He had never greeted or talked to me before. Not realizing my dad was watching from the side apartment window of my bedroom, to my surprise and chagrin, I heard the window slide open. My dad stuck his head out, and in a rage, yelled at this boy to stay away from me and to never talk to me again!

I wanted to hide in disgrace and shame. I was only being polite in acknowledging his greeting. I had no interest in pursuing a friendship with this boy, nor any interest or liking for him—nor any other boy for that matter!

Embarrassed and humiliated, I tried explaining to my dad when I got home that he was a student from school who happened to walk the same path as me. My heart throbbed with fear, but I was also saddened by being falsely accused of having friendship with a *boy*. Imagine: me with a boy! Had my parents seen this boy walking near me before, and assumed we were friends? Perhaps my dad was preparing to break that friendship?

Not unexpectedly, I never saw that boy walk home that way again! I feared I would be made fun of, but there were no repercussions at school and no one found out.

After that, whenever I approached the dreaded apartment window I would slow down and look around to make sure no males were near me before I passed by. I did not want my dad to have another opportunity to shout at anyone else, nor to re-experience the hurt of being suspected of unfaithfulness.

Sometimes when we were working on a group project, the teacher required the students to exchange home telephone numbers. I *had* to give my phone number to the group, while at the same time anticipating what could happen if I ever received a phone call from a boy in the group. Losing concentration and focus, with my stomach in knots, my heart racing, and my palms sweaty, I would get short of breath thinking of the outcome. It was not worth being scolded for talking to a boy or having a boy call me at home. Besides, many of them were dumber than me and always acted stupid and said ridiculous things. Best stay clear of them!

Entering grade nine—high school—the following year was a big step. It was the largest brick school building I had ever seen. It was overwhelming for me, compared to our small elementary school, to vanish in the masses. It meant there were more students to stare at my awkwardness. I did not belong with the girls who dressed beyond their age, in designer skintight jeans with their pretty tops laced in jewelry and nice hairdos and faces lavished with makeup.

I must have appeared like a poor misfit to most of my classmates. My clothes did not fit well, as my wardrobe consisted of baggy old jeans, which I wore every day. I tried stitching the sides to tighten them around my skinny legs, just like the other girls did, but after one wash, the threads came apart. Noticing the loose threads hanging off my jeans brought my mother distress as she tried to understand what I was up to. Eventually she figured out that I was trying to tighten my jeans. After some scolding, I knew I would not be able to try that again without being caught by her.

The accompanying worn out mock turtle-neck sweater hung loosely, with the neck so stretched out of shape that it no longer sat neatly. Sometimes I would put an elastic band around my neck to hold it up, which I learned from girls who used elastic bands to keep their socks up. Once a boy sitting behind me noticed the elastic peeking from under the cuff of the neck, and in astonishment, he tapped my shoulder to tell me how dangerous it was to put an elastic around my neck! This made me self-conscious, but it didn't stop me—I just made sure to conceal the elastic more carefully. The sweater's sleeves, which were once at wrist level, now crawled halfway up my arms. Both the back and front of this sweater needed constant pulling down to cover any skin peeking beyond the waist band of the jeans whenever I sat down in class. It was the only sweater I had, now a few sizes too small. The only consolation was that it was a bright aqua.

My running shoes were completely worn out, with the bottom sole detaching and flapping as I walked. The hole at the big toe allowed rainwater to soak my socks. It was not unusual for me to sit with wet feet throughout the school day. Once a year, I would get either a new pair of shoes or jeans for my birthday.

The local barber continued to cut my hair, although he complained that I should go to a woman's hair salon, for which he politely gave me directions. Despite his unwillingness and embarrassment, he quietly removed all excess hair to a boyish haircut. He knew my mother demanded it, or else she would send me back in dissatisfaction and make him further crop my hair. Eventually, I refused to get my hair cut short, and I was allowed to keep it at shoulder length.

Sometimes girls sitting next to me in class would offer me used mascara or blush, which I would hide in my pencil case. With my mother's frequent surveillance of my desk at home, the makeup would inevitably be found—to her horror. Loud, angry words would erupt out of her mouth as she trashed everything, only to prompt me to start my collection again as girls continued to pass on their old makeup. Sometimes, with lunch donut money put aside, I would go to a drug store and purchase makeup to lighten my skin colour by several shades. *If I look lighter, I probably will be accepted by my peers,* I thought, *since most students in the school are white.* The staring got worse, undoubtedly, when students saw my fake blanched face.

In addition to makeup, marijuana joints were also passed around in class. One girl sitting next to me always seem to have some available in her jean pocket to pass around like candy. I would refuse each time, but the girl, Joanne, made several attempts anyway. We had learned about the dangers of drugs from our elementary school principal, Mr. Robertson, in grade seven. This girl would also offer me cigarettes. I never accepted these, either, but that didn't stop her from trying again and again. *I do not want to smell like her,* I thought.

My parents still did not allow me to associate with anyone outside of school. No one called me on the phone or rang our doorbell. At this time in a young person's life, when self-esteem is so important, I had *none*.

The Son of man [Jesus]… a friend of publicans and sinners! (Luke 7:34)

Chapter 26

DEPRESSION

The LORD is nigh [near] unto them that
are of a broken heart; and saveth such as
be of a contrite spirit.
(Psalm 34:18)

One day, my Aunt Alka, my mother's youngest sister, arrived
at our place after a visit to India. Among other things, she
brought us jars of mango and lime pickles like my grandmother
used to make in Kenya. Indulging from the first jar, both my
mother and I got ill. We were not sure if the jars had not been
properly sealed, the food was too old, or deficient hygiene prac-
tices had been used to make it, but we both got the same bowel
symptoms at the same time. After taking a round of prescribed
antibiotics, both my mother and I developed an allergic reaction
to the medication. Our skin started itching, followed by severe,
unsightly peeling all over our bodies. It was bizarre, and I was
self-conscious to even expose my hands in school.

My dad decided to take both of us to the doctor. In my presence, the doctor explained to my dad that the illness was a *viral*
disease, occurring from contamination from food we had eaten.

Arriving home, I noticed my parents whispering to each other,
while my mother glared at me in abhorrence. My dad took me

aside and stated with disgust that I had *venereal* disease! What I read in his face and heard in his words stung deeply in my heart. He assumed I was having sex with boys at school. I thought, *I never talk to boys and stay clear of them in obedience to my parents, and he thinks I have venereal disease!* How was this even possible? I always came straight home from school and was never allowed to go out with friends! Shocked, I questioned him further: why would the doctor say such a thing when my mother and I had the *same* symptoms? Then he said that the doctor made this statement in front of me!

"No, he did not," I said, bewildered, with the little air left in me. "The doctor said *viral* disease—a disease from a *virus*, not *venereal* disease. Call the doctor and ask him to clarify!" In desperation, I demanded and pleaded with my father for the first time. In their phone conversation, the doctor was stunned that what he had said was interpreted so wrongly. "No, she does not have venereal disease, she has a *viral* disease!" My dad repeated his words to me, and no apologies were made.

This was one of the most excruciatingly painful days of my young life—to have my parents accuse me, and not believe anything I said. My words held no value. It took the doctor's words to make things right. My parents had no confidence in my character. The hurt lasted for days, then years, deeply etched into my memory— the horror of being wrongfully accused, even though I tried so hard to *please* them. I suffered in private once again, pondering this in my head repeatedly. My heart stayed wounded.

Once again, my dignity fell a further few notches. I felt numb and could not express the feelings in words to myself. I did not even want to talk to myself about it. It was deplorable that not only was there no *love* in this home for me, but my parents did not *trust* me. Instead, they imagined my character to be immoral and rebellious. Committing such an act of defiance would not just have been against my parents' values, but against the values and convictions that I held *myself!* I did not want to have sex with boys!

Then this same aunt, Alka, commented to my mother how I resembled her other sister, Reena. This was the sister my mother *despised:* the fairer sister who had moved to England, who my mother refused to have contact with, and to whom she did not want me to continue writing letters. I felt upset at hearing these comments, but did not show it to anyone. I knew there was still another reason my mother loathed me: because I resembled a sister she hated!

I already didn't feel I had a strong family bond with my parents and brother. What made matters worse was that my mother's obvious show of love and favouritism for my brother *increased.* I was distressed, but also felt provoked with envy and jealousy. The void in my heart from loneliness at home used to be filled by teachers and friends caring for me. Now, at the new school, I could not even rely on them for support.

My deteriorating emotional and physical health got me increasingly depressed. I still had a weak stomach, and frequently got bouts of bronchitis. But now the severe monthly ovarian pain took precedence, making normal functioning more difficult. Sometimes I would leave class and agonize in the school washroom, keeled over in pain and self-conscious if anyone walked in.

Being uncomfortable and insecure with my outward appearance when I went to school, I felt like I did not belong *anywhere!* I looked so thin and unhappy. My small wardrobe didn't amount to much: either the clothes didn't fit well, or I wore the same ones repeatedly.

We had no relatives staying in Canada, other than my uncle in Toronto. The rare visits of some aunts and uncles from Kenya added some dimension to home life, as my parents seemed to come alive after spending hours at the kitchen table sharing stories. But even with their visits, my life was boring, meaningless, and lonely.

I often thought about my grandmother after we left Kenya, but memories of her became even more vivid during these dark days. I tried to fixate on her to give me comfort and to have something positive to focus on. The greatest blow of all was that I had no one, not even a grandmother, to buffer the blows of life as a young growing teenager. The emotional pain was becoming more raw and intense as I desired my grandmother's presence more and more, the love I once used to know—my *definition* of love. But now the pain was so great that even a grandmother's love couldn't alleviate it: the pain of utter emptiness, worthlessness, loneliness, and hopelessness. I wondered if a person could survive without love. I had lost my worth and dignity as a human being, and the drive to live was gone.

There was a vacuum in my heart. Darkness enveloped me as I stood alone in its grips. It cast me down so low that a cloud of depression and isolation took over me, compressing me lower and lower into the ground, into a deep pit all alone. I no longer had a reason to live, or an expectation that I might be rescued; I had no motivation to crawl out.

Ideas came to mind, occupying my thoughts with ways to kill myself. Drug overdose or cutting my wrists? At the age of thirteen, I wanted to *die*.

From the end of the earth will I cry unto thee, when my heart is overwhelmed: lead me to the rock that is higher than I. (Psalm 61:2)

…that Rock was Christ. (1 Corinthians 10:4)

Chapter 27

CALLING OUT TO AN UNKNOWN GOD

> She weepeth sore in the night,
> and her tears are on her cheeks…
> she hath none to comfort her…
> (Lamentations 1:2)

> I am weary with my groaning;
> all the night make I my bed to swim;
> I water my couch with my tears.
> (Psalm 6:6)

The apartment was quiet; everyone else was fast asleep. My brother, in our narrow and dark bedroom, slept soundly on the bunk bed below. My parents could not be heard, except for the occasional loud snore from my dad interrupting the stillness.

All were oblivious to the raging battle of sorrow and pain inside of me that night. I had reached a climactic point when I finally needed to admit to myself that I was experiencing a downward spiral and hitting rock bottom. My heart carried agonizing pain, and there was no escape. I needed to face the truth of my abandonment, loneliness, and unworthiness. The struggle was real. My life had no value—I had no value. No one cared or even noticed that I mattered or existed. I was a prisoner trapped in my circumstances, unable to be free.

No one knew about my nightly ritual of soaking the pillow with my tears as I relived the hurts I had felt during the day. But this momentous night was by far the *worst*. I became conscious of having no hope, nor any reason to live. Various methods came to mind to end my life. Would I overdose myself with the medicine in the cabinet or slash my wrists? Suicidal thoughts only brought me to perceive my impoverished and helpless state.

I discovered for the first time in my life the depth of my need. It was so great that no human could avail such pain. The pain was so intense that even my grandmother would not have been able to heal it. Turning to my religion, I felt it had failed me—the gods were so distant, and they didn't care. In some of his stories about India, my dad had even said that the gods needed to be appeased by extreme self-denial and sacrifices. So profound was my agony that my cry was no longer to the male and female Hindu gods.

As I lay in the dark, tears flowed and I wiped them on my pillow. I continued to cry silently, hoping no one in the apartment would hear me. I remained as motionless as I could to make sure my brother would not wake up. My need was deep, and my pain was real. Deprived and destitute, I knew my emotional condition was beyond human help.

For the second time in my early life, I had a sense of *Someone* listening to me as I cried out. At the age of thirteen, in the only way that I could express how I was feeling, I asked this *Unknown Stranger* to "Make me into a bird so I can fly away!"

I wept softly, with tears rolling down my face. I wanted to be loosened from the restraints that caged me in a life so miserable, so lonely, and so hopeless. My cry was deliberate and forceful. I had reached the end of myself, and in my desperation, I continued to hopelessly weep in the cold, shadowy room.

And I said, Oh that I had wings like a dove! for then would
I fly away, and be at rest. (Psalm 55:6)

Heartbroken, having reached my limit, I was unable to escape
from this trap of despair. In desperation, again I made my plea in
the dark, lonely room, whispering for fear of waking the family. I
wanted to be free of all my circumstances and troubles.

I pleaded with the Stranger several times to be made into a
bird so I could fly away. I cried like I had never cried before. I told
Him I knew He could make me into a bird, because I believed He
could, so why was He not doing it? Who was this Person I was
talking to Who remained so silent?

My soul longeth, yea, even fainteth for the courts of the
LORD: my heart and my flesh crieth out for the *living God*.
(Psalm 84:2, emphasis added)

My soul thirsteth for God, for the *living God...* (Psalm
42:2, emphasis added)

Silence. Out of utter emotional exhaustion, I fell asleep on the
pillow, now drenched on both sides.

This crucial night proved later to be a turning point in my
life. Remarkably and unknowingly, I was calling out to the *God*
in *Heaven!* The freedom I longed for would have to come from
Someone powerful, compassionate, and caring enough to pull me
out of the deep pit of hopelessness and allow me to fly free as a
bird.

The trust I wanted others to have in me, and the value and
love I desperately required, were lacking in my home life. The
freedom to communicate and express my feelings was neglected.
Although I was in a pathetic state, God was in absolute control of

my destiny and had devised an eternal plan He would soon unfold by His power and wisdom!

> Jesus saith unto her, Woman, why weepest thou? *whom seekest thou?* (John 20:15, emphasis added)

> Come unto me [Jesus], all ye that labour and are heavy laden, and I will give you rest. (Matthew 11:28)

Chapter 28

FINDING A LITTLE TREASURE

O God, thou art my God; early will I
seek thee: *my soul thirsteth
for thee*, my flesh longeth for thee in a dry
and thirsty land, where no water is…
(Psalm 63:1, emphasis added)

After that desperate night of crying, life seemed more miserable. However, the humbling experience continued to provoke me to a realization and an admission of my condition: a broken spirit and a lonely, empty heart. I had no one to share my thoughts or feelings with, so *alone* I carried this burden.

One morning on the way to my high school, I decided to take a short-cut through a laneway. As I approached an elementary schoolyard, the loud squeals of laughter and the happy voices of children playing behind a tall chain-link fence distracted me from my sad, heavy heart.

As I walked along the concrete pathway, I suddenly had an incredible urge to pick up *something* off the ground. Oddly, I had not seen anything in front of me! As I bent down, I picked up a little red booklet two and a half by two inches in size. Placing it carefully into my pocket, I continued walking towards school, excited to have found a little treasure.

I never read books under my desk like the other students did, abiding by the rules of the classroom, but this book seemed different. I was *eager* to read it. I carefully leaned the booklet against the lower shelf of the desk and read the cover, *Little Bible*, and then flipped open the crisp new pages. I placed it cautiously in the front pocket of my jeans to be read at home.

That night, as I lay in bed, I began to read the inside cover. "Keep this book and read it daily." *I will*, I thought to Whoever instructed me to do so. With great enthusiasm, I began to read the precious Words. The first verse seemed like a command: *"…blessed are they that hear the word of God, and keep it"* (Luke 11:28).

Nightly, I read this *Little Bible* from cover to cover, trying to decipher the meaning of its unique Words. During the day, I carried it in my jeans pocket everywhere I went. Daily, the Words of the *Little Bible* gave me comfort and strength.

> *Thy words were found,* and I did eat them; and thy word was unto me the joy and rejoicing of mine heart: for I am called by thy name, O Lord God of hosts. (Jeremiah 15:16, emphasis added)

One day, as I lay sick in bed, my mother noticed me clutching the little red booklet in my hand. Instead of asking about it, she broke out in laugher at the absurdity. Loudly, she shared the news with my dad that I was sick and was holding onto a little book in my hand!

> My soul melteth for heaviness: strengthen thou me according unto *thy word.* (Psalm 119:28, emphasis added)

One fateful day, I forgot to remove my *Little Bible* from my pocket before I put it in the wash. What I saw shocked and disappointed me. Not only was the cover of the booklet soaking wet, but the pages inside fell apart into small pieces that I could not separate. Hanging my head in anguish as I looked at the shredded bits of my precious booklet in my hands, I felt my life had come to a halt! *What should I do now?* I thought.

As was my nightly custom, I lay in bed without my booklet, trying to remember the Words. This time, to my astonishment, as I recited the first verse, I noticed how the rest of the verses flowed by memory. Those powerful Words were inscribed into my mind, but I felt that Someone greater than I had inscribed them into my heart!

In an amazing transformation, my heart was touched by the powerful Words spoken by Someone so Great. Psalm 50:15 was one verse I recited continually, telling me that if I was to call upon Him in the day of trouble, He would deliver me. Another powerful verse told me that if I would seek Him with all my heart, I would find Him (Jeremiah 29:13). Every night, my soul was calm and peaceful. My pillow was no longer wet. I no longer had thoughts of death or suicide. I now had a sense of *peace*—a *peace* I had never experienced before, the source of which I could not understand!

> I will both lay me down *in peace,* and sleep: for thou, LORD, only makest me dwell in safety. (Psalm 4:8, emphasis added)

> ...the *peace of God,* which passeth all understanding... (Philippians 4:7, emphasis added)

This was the start of a *new chapter* in my life, which I did not realize at the time; nor did I understand what it would encompass!

The Lord God had methodically removed all distractions and protective cushioning to empty me, so I would feel my need of Him. He had planned that I would find that booklet on the laneway at the precise time when my heart was ready to receive His Words. The timing was perfect as the ground of my heart had been plowed. Those Words—powerful, life-changing, comforting, inspired by God Himself—were healing to an aching heart and a soul struggling to find hope and reason to life. God came in to help during my frantic struggles, pouring in balm with the Words He spoke. I had no head knowledge of what I was reading about salvation; I did not know this Person Jesus. But those Words spoke peace and security and a calmness to my hungry, thirsty, and barren soul.

My mother did not recognize the value of the *Little Bible*—so precious that it renewed the life of her daughter, contemplating suicide. Her neglect and her abandonment of me provoked the Almighty God to take me up first by giving me a taste of His Word, and more was yet to come!

Thou art my hiding place and my shield: I hope in thy word. (Psalm 119:114)

Thy word is a *lamp* unto my feet, and a *light* unto my path. (Psalm 119:105, emphasis added)

Chapter 29

ONE SCHOOL FRIEND

For I am poor and needy,
and *my heart is wounded within me.*
(Psalm 109:22, emphasis added)

Unlike the rest of the girls at high school, I did not wear any jewellery or makeup. My wardrobe still consisted of clothing which I outgrew—a blouse and a pair of jeans renewed at each birthday. My canvas running shoes still had to last the year. Being poorly dressed for the cold winters was something I needed to get used to. I felt neglected in every aspect of my growing up years but remained silent, as complaining was never an option.

A girl named Susan had been my classmate in elementary school, although we had never talked to each other very much. She was shy and kept to herself, and didn't hang around the same girls I did. She was an average student who never had her work highlighted in front of the class, nor did the rest of the students accept her as a popular girl. From the way she dressed—mismatched wrinkled clothes—I assumed she was poor. Her most noticeable features were her big brown laughing eyes and her wide, happy smile, which showed off her large, protruding ivory teeth. Her stark white skin contrasted with her messy black pigtails, which always had tufts of hair coming out in all directions, making her appear more juvenile.

On the way to high school, many mornings I would approach Susan to walk alongside her. I assumed she also had no friends, as I always saw her alone in the corridors. Our conversations were superficial and boring, *but* she was a *friend*. It turned out that she was in my homeroom and French class.

Our daily routine, after eating our modest lunch, was to head for the library to complete schoolwork. We worked silently, but for some of the students, this was a time for socializing. As the volume of conversation escalated, the librarian would visit each desk to tell everyone to lower their voices. When news got around that the library was too noisy to complete assignments, our French teacher announced we could go to her classroom during the lunch hour for "study time." I thought it was a great idea, so I tried convincing my friend to accompany me.

After I repeatedly asked Susan one day to go to our French teacher's class to complete our homework, she seemed annoyed with me and walked away. Being somewhat reluctant myself, I passed by the classroom, wanting to look inside. There were people sitting in a circle, and I heard someone call out to me to come inside. Embarrassed that I had been noticed, I decided to walk in. I was given a chair. As I sat very still, I awkwardly and politely listened to someone in the group reading out of a large burgundy book, presumably the Bible, none of which I understood. *What happened to the lunch study time?* I thought.

The teacher must have assumed I wanted to come to *Bible* study. At the end of the session, I privately shared with her that I had found a little pocket Bible, which I had lost in the wash. She said she was familiar with the booklet and would provide me with another. Ecstatic, knowing my lost *Treasure* could be replaced, I thanked her. However, on receiving the booklet one day after class, I noticed it was in *French!* Finding it difficult to read, I disappointedly put it away in my desk.

My French teacher invited me to her church events numerous times. But after a while, assuming that I was not interested, she stopped contacting me. I had *expected* this would happen eventually. I was reserved and shy, and had difficulty expressing the restrictions I had in my personal life. She was also unaware of my background, and my cultural and religious restrictions. This saddened me, as I liked her gentle and serene nature and the attention she had given me for that short time.

My classmate Susan hung out with me for a while but soon gave up, as we did not have common school interests. I found her boring, and she must have felt the same about me. Even though our friendship was short, I still felt abandoned by the *only* friend I had in high school.

…his compassions fail not. They are new every morning: *great is thy faithfulness.* (Lamentations 3:22–23, emphasis added)

Chapter 30

MOVING TO THE SUBURBS

The LORD is good unto them that wait
for him, to the soul that seeketh him. It
is good that a man should both *hope and
quietly wait for the salvation of the LORD*.
(Lamentations 3:25–26, emphasis added)

In Grade Ten, my parents decided to buy a house in a suburban area. We had to be bused half an hour east to the biggest high school I had ever seen. It was newer than my previous high school, with twice the number of students, mostly from middle-class families.

Social life was still uneventful for me, even here. Once again, I made the effort to make friends and be sociable, but inevitably only had superficial relationships—except for Linda. She was smart but odd. Her hair was *too* perfectly curled in at the bottom ends. Often, in our conversations, she would make sure it stayed curled in, fiddling nervously with her hands. We got along fine as both of us did well in school. However, knowing I was getting higher marks than her in biology—in fact, the highest in the class—she decided to mock my ultra-detailed pen and pastel drawings of a yellow perch fish and a dissected frog, saying it was a waste of time that I should spend so much time on art. After all, it was biology class, not art class. She did not know that that was all I did at home: homework and drawing! This revealed a side of her I did not like. She was jealous of my accomplishments!

After that, I kept a comfortable distance from Linda, except for receiving stupid notes in class about a "talking amoeba." I would politely write back with a dumb comment, still secretly wanting a friend—*any* friend.

I was grateful that Linda's parents picked me up for the high school graduation; otherwise, I would not have been able to attend the ceremony, as my parents refused to go. Everyone was silent in the car. Her parents indiscreetly asked me about my family. I awkwardly told them my sister was sick in bed.

When I arrived back home after the ceremony, no one fussed or asked to see the red hardcover book displaying my diploma.

Walking into my room, I saw my sister laying on the bed looking even *sicker*. She appeared to be having difficulty breathing, with her nostrils flaring out! I immediately convinced my dad that he must take her to the nearest hospital. Once we arrived, the emergency doctor informed my dad that my sister had not only pneumonia, but bronchitis too. Her oxygen saturation was low, so they gave her oxygen with her bed enclosed in a tent. I overheard the doctor tell my dad that I had saved my sister's life by having brought her to the hospital in time!

Linda wanted us to play tennis after graduation, but I could never express that I was not allowed to go out. Our friendship dwindled when she moved away to New York State for university. I missed her.

In math, my favourite subject, I noticed that the East Indian teacher would always let the class know the highest mark of one male East Indian student, who would beat me only by a few points, but never mentioned when my score was the highest. He would stare at me uncomfortably as he made the announcement, knowing very well he never pointed out my perfect exam results. Instead of fighting to retain my score, I gave up and let the boy get the math award at graduation. This teacher annoyed me with his sexism, but I always regretted I gave up so easily.

One day, a classmate sitting in front of me turned around and subtly mentioned that his friend preferred quiet girls and liked getting to know them. I knew who he was referring to, and I looked over to a student facing us with his back to the side wall. My immediate response was not to flinch or show any emotion. The response they would both read was that I was not interested. I was left alone, to my relief, but at the same time flattered someone had noticed me.

I lost attentiveness in school, as many of the teachers taught poorly or not at all. The French teacher was drug-intoxicated in class, and none of us knew how to handle this recurrent situation. Chemistry class was taught by a teacher who wore a white lab coat and always seemed to talk under her breath to cover up what she did not know, and never taught us the material necessary to prepare for the year-end exam. She retired the next year. English class was a social time to apply what we knew in essays. Physics was straight out of the textbook, taught by a teacher with a such a strong Egyptian accent that we could hardly follow him. My present science program would allow me to apply for health sciences in college and continue into university. Everyone seemed to follow the same course of attending college, then university, most not really having any specific goals.

Relatives would come and go. Home life was relatively quiet. Interactions with my parents happened only when I was asked to do chores like take care of the gardens, plant the vegetables, mow the lawn, apply wallpaper, paint the house inside and outside, or shovel the snow. Sometimes I was to tutor my sister in math and English for the whole summer. I had to file and organize all my dad's documents. I was asked to help remove wallpaper and paint at several of my uncle's investment properties and to do body work on one of his cars.

At odd times, my brother would flash his bank book at me to show the money he was given for working for our uncle, which I never got. This angered and upset me, but I kept quiet, and wondered why he needed to be so *mean*. For the most part, I was alone at home with my sister for the summer months. My brother would take summer courses, so he was never home. Both my parents would leave early for work in the city and return at supper time.

I started a two-year science program at a college. Commuting by bus for two hours, then walking for some distance to the campus, took a lot longer than travelling with my parents by car. To save money and time, I often traveled with them.

At college registration, the teacher teaching an Honours Calculus course was trying to influence as many students as he could to take his course; otherwise, he would receive no funding for lack of students. I was already in Honours Biology and had a good enough grade, so he convinced me to take the class. I did not enjoy theoretical calculus or the textbook by Michael Spivak, which made my head spin. I asked the instructor to remove me from the class, but he again persuaded me that my marks were adequate. *Next term, I will not enroll in the second part of this boring course,* I thought. To my dismay, I was once again convinced to take the course by the instructor.

It was in this class that I met Sandra, a good student. We often sat together and discussed homework assignments. It was a class of strong students, some wanting to apply into the medical program. At this time, Sandra and I never met outside of class.

...the Son of man [Jesus] is come to seek and to save that which was lost. (Luke 19:10)

...the kindness and love of God our Saviour toward man appeared... (Titus 3:4)

Chapter 31

SALVATION!

The LORD hath made known his salvation:
his righteousness hath he openly shewed
in the sight of the heathen.
(Psalm 98:2, emphasis added)

At the age of eighteen, for the *first time* in my life, my dad and I sat in the living room every Saturday afternoon to watch a specific television program. It was hosted by the leader of a large organization (which was considered a cult in Christian circles, although I did not know that at the time). Topics included politics, poverty, wars, and hunger in the world. After each show, my dad and I would discuss world issues and give our own philosophical views and thoughts about the subjects.

On one of the episodes, the host talked about Jesus Christ as a historical figure Who once walked on the earth. At the end of the show, he advertised that he was sending out free literature about the life of Christ, as depicted in the books Matthew, Mark, Luke, and John.

Instantly, this sparked an interest and a curiosity in me; I wanted to write to him to find out *Who this Jesus was.*

That I may know him [Jesus]… (Philippians 3:10)

I began to seek for One Who had already had His eye on me all along, and His promise was that I would find Him if I searched for Him with all my heart. These were the verses that also had an impact on me from the *Little Bible,* and which I often recited:

Seek ye the LORD while he may be found, call ye upon him while he is near… (Isaiah 55:6, emphasis added)

And ye shall seek me, and find me, when ye shall search for me with all your heart. (Jeremiah 29:13, emphasis added)

The following days, I could not stop thinking about the program I had watched with my dad. I remembered that the host had mentioned that this *Jesus* was talked about in the Bible. I wondered where I could get a copy of the Bible. I also remembered another verse from the *Little Bible,* where it said that He would not cast me away if I came to Him:

All that the Father giveth me shall come to me; and him that cometh to me I will in *no wise cast out.* (John 6:37, emphasis added)

On the way to college, I entered a nearby mall to look for a bookstore, hoping to purchase a Bible. As I got to the bookstore counter, I felt ashamed and uncomfortable that as a Hindu, I was asking for a Bible. The clerk directed me to the back of the store, where there were huge, expensive family Bibles on display. I did not have enough money, so I left the store empty-handed. I pondered for days how I could possibly get a copy of the Bible to read during the four-month summer break from college, as I was not allowed to get a job.

Blessed is the man *whom thou choosest,* and causest to approach unto thee, that he may dwell in thy courts: we shall be satisfied with the *goodness of thy house,* even of thy holy temple. (Psalm 65:4, emphasis added)

At the end of the school semester, I made one last trip accompanying my parents in their car to check if my final marks had been posted at the college.

As I walked towards the college campus, I approached an intersection, where I met Sandra from my Honours Calculus class. She informed me that the marks were not yet posted, so she invited me to come to her house nearby to spend the rest of the afternoon. As I needed to wait till the end of the day to meet up with my parents to return home anyway, I thought this would be a good idea. I knew my parents would not have liked me going to someone else's house, but I had some troubling questions which I thought Sandra may be able to answer for me.

I will rise now, and go about the city in the streets, and in the broad ways I will seek him whom my soul loveth: *I sought him,* but I found him not. (Song of Solomon 3:2, emphasis added)

What I really wanted was for her to answer my questions about *God!* I asked her as we walked to her home if she believed in God, and she said she did. Satisfied with the reply, I became excited to get some more answers, so I assured myself this was the right thing to do.

When we got to her place, I asked her once again if she believed in God. But this time, she questioned me: "Who is God and where is He anyway?" I was *horrified* to realize she did not believe in God after all. Unexpectedly reacting with bold certainty, I blurted out: "God said, *'I AM that I AM!'*"

I astonished myself, as I was not conscious of knowing such a fact. Feeling nervous, I started defending myself that it was in the Bible. My friend Sandra, looking mad about being challenged, ran upstairs to get a copy of the Bible to prove me wrong.

...O LORD God of hosts, cause *thy face to shine;* and we shall be *saved.* (Psalm 80:19, emphasis added)

As I stood looking out the large window, I felt the warmth of the sunlight flooding into the room and into my heart as I realized at that moment that something *great* was about to happen!

Surely his salvation is nigh them that fear him; that glory may dwell in our land. (Psalm 85:9)

Sandra interrupted my thoughts as she entered the room, handing me a Bible. I appreciated how big the Bible really was as I flipped the pages back and forth, trying to find the verse that I assumed was in it. I kept saying, "It is in here somewhere!"

Thrilled to see a Bible in my hands, I asked her where to get a copy. She went back upstairs, and as she returned, making her way down the stairs, she proudly announced that she had been awarded this Bible at Sunday school as a prize and that I could *have it.* I told her my parents would not allow me to keep a Bible, but I would just borrow it to read in the summer and return it to her in the fall.

So then *faith* cometh by hearing, and hearing by *the word of God.* (Romans 10:17, emphasis added)

I left Sandra's home eagerly with a pocket-size Gideon New Testament in hand. I recognized that the burgundy cover was like that of the copy I had received annually at the elementary school—the one that would mysteriously disappear from inside my desk, likely ending up in the garbage. This time I would be able to read it!

> It was but a little that I passed from them, but *I found him whom my soul loveth:* I held him, and would not let him go, until I had brought him into my mother's house...
> (Song of Solomon 3:4, emphasis added)

On taking the New Testament home, I decided to leave it in full view on the top of my dresser. I wanted to make sure my parents knew I had a Bible in my possession and would be reading it. No sooner had I placed it there, when my parents walked in and got very upset to see a Bible in my room. I told them it was *just* to read it in the summer, and that I would return it back to my friend. Although they were troubled, my parents reluctantly allowed me to keep the Bible for the summer. What they did not realize was the power of the Word of God to save a soul!!

> For *the word of God is quick, and powerful, and sharper than any twoedged sword,* piercing even to the dividing asunder of soul and spirit, and of the joints and marrow, and is a discerner of the thoughts and intents of the heart.
> (Hebrews 4:12, emphasis added)

In the days following, being home alone, I began to read Matthew, Mark, and Luke from the New Testament. The Words of power exploded out of the precious pages as I drank in each one. My heart burned within me as I learned about this Glorious Person!

> …Did not our heart burn within us, while he talked with us by the way, and while *he opened to us the scriptures?* (Luke 24:32, emphasis added)

I read about a magnificent Person born into this world by a miraculous virgin birth, worshipped by both shepherds and wise men. I read about One with such great power that He could perform incredible miracles: raising people from the dead, opening the eyes of the blind, opening the ears of the deaf, healing the lame and sick, and removing demons from those who were possessed. I read about One displaying His splendour in kindness and love to the unlovely and reaching out in compassion to individuals searching for the Truth. I read about the grandeur and uniqueness of His power to forgive sins. From reading each of the three gospels, I also read about a hateful, jealous mob who pronounced judgment on this meek, gentle, and perfect One Who called Himself the Son of God. I was awestruck at His submission to the hands of wicked men about to commit a horrific act. I read about His torturous, humiliating, and suffering death. I read about His incredible resurrection from the dead on the third day, as He had prophesied.

> Jesus answered… the works that I do in my Father's name, they bear *witness of me.* (John 10:25, emphasis added)

Overwhelmed as I read from the precious little Book about this wonderful Person, my heart cried within me, wanting to meet Him! I had never read or heard about a human being *so beautiful!*

As I got to the book of John, I did not even realize what was happening, but *"...Jesus himself drew near..."* (Luke 24:15), and I saw *"no man, save Jesus only"* (Matthew 17:8).

Then *opened he their understanding,* that they might *understand the scriptures...* (Luke 24:45, emphasis added)

My understanding was opened. My heart was full of unmeasurable joy as I fell in love with this glorious Man and God I was meeting for the first time: the Lord Jesus Christ, the Son of God!

My beloved is... the chiefest among ten thousand... his... countenance... excellent... His mouth is most sweet: yea, he is altogether lovely. This is my beloved, and this is my friend... (Song of Solomon 5:10–16)

I recognized my need as a sinner and accepted the Lord Jesus Christ as my Saviour! For the first time in my life, the tears I shed were from the abundance of joy and adoration for the new Truth which I now knew: *Jesus Christ!*

A passage having a dramatic impact on me was:

He that hath my commandments, and keepeth them, he it is that loveth me: and he that loveth me shall be loved of my Father, and I will love him, and will *manifest myself to him...*

Jesus answered and said unto him, If a man love me, he will keep my words: and my Father will love him, and we will come unto him, and *make our abode with him.* (John 14:21, 23, emphasis added)

The Lord Jesus did indeed manifest Himself, and I felt His awesome Presence with me. I recognized that the *familiar voice* from the Words in the *Little Bible* which I had found when I was thirteen was this same Jesus I now met at the age of eighteen, in 1977. Not only was He speaking to me from His Word, the Holy Scriptures, but He made me discern that He was indeed the Lord Jesus Himself!

> Jesus saith unto her, *I that speak unto thee am he.* (John 4:26, emphasis added)

> ...that disciple whom Jesus loved saith... *It is the Lord.* (John 21:7, emphasis added)

I fell to my knees and worshipped Him for saving my life and saving me as a sinner. I thanked Him for having cared for me those past years as an Unseen Visitor.

For the first time in my life, I felt an unexplained sense of freedom and peace so deep that it filled me with an amazing joy unspeakable! It was the fulfilment of what my heart had been longing for all those years. It was the True God Himself, the Only One Who could truly satisfy me! The Living God giving me the privilege of having an intimate relationship with Him!

> ...whosoever drinketh of the water that I shall give him shall never thirst; but the water that I shall give him shall be in him a well of water springing up into *everlasting life.* (John 4:14, emphasis added)

It was God the Father Who revealed His Beloved Son to me through the work of the Holy Spirit ministering the Word, the Scriptures, to my heart. It was He Who was searching for me in His great love and compassion through the work of the Holy Spirit in my life! The various circumstances I went through made my need so great in preparing my heart to receive Him.

> In whom ye also trusted, after that ye heard *the word of truth,* the *gospel of your salvation:* in whom also after that ye believed, ye were sealed with that holy Spirit of promise… (Ephesians 1:13, emphasis added)

A story comes to mind from Luke 13 about a woman suffering with a *"spirit of infirmity"* for eighteen years. Whether the illness was mental, physical, or spiritual is not clear. She was *"bowed together"* and didn't have the ability to lift herself up. A Source outside of herself was the only One to help and rescue her!

> And, behold, there was a woman which had *a spirit of infirmity eighteen years,* and was bowed together, and could in no wise lift up herself. (Luke 13:11, emphasis added)

The Lord Jesus saw her, noticed her predicament, and called her to Him. How awesome! We see displayed His character of sympathy and compassion as He reached out to a lowly, helpless woman. His Words of power spoken in Divine authority declared the healing of this woman: *"And when Jesus saw her, he called her to him, and said unto her, <u>Woman, thou art loosed from thine infirmity</u>"* (Luke 13:12, emphasis added).

He spoke to her and laid His hands on her, and the woman was immediately made straight and healed! *"And he laid his hands on her: and immediately she was <u>made straight,</u> and <u>glorified God</u>"* (Luke 13:13, emphasis added).

Her response was to glorify God in gratitude. The Lord Jesus stated that she had been bound for eighteen years by Satan: *"The*

Lord... said... ought not this woman... whom Satan hath bound, lo, these <u>eighteen years, be loosed from this bond</u>... " (Luke 13:15, 16, emphasis added).

I could relate with this woman: bound by Satan for eighteen years, unable to help myself. The Lord Jesus, reaching out to me in compassion, love, grace, and mercy, released me from the bondage of Hinduism. I was bound by thoughts of my unworthiness, my unloveliness, my skin colour, my lack of value as a woman, and my lack of merit as a human being. Like this woman, my desire was (and is) also to glorify Him. She was helpless and unable to rescue herself, very much like I was, needing Someone outside of my strength to lift me up out of a pit of clay.

> He brought me up also out of an horrible pit, out of the miry clay, and *set my feet upon a rock,* and established my goings. (Psalm 40:2, emphasis added)

> I love them that love me; and those that seek me early shall find me. (Proverbs 8:17)

I did not realize *my true value as a child of God,* my value and worth, and that my Lord Jesus was a King, till I read Psalm 45:10–11:

> Hearken, *O daughter,* and consider, and incline thine ear; forget also thine own people, and thy father's house; So shall *the king greatly desire thy beauty: for he is thy Lord;* and worship thou him. (emphasis added)

The promise of the work of the Lord Jesus Christ on the cross to redeem sinners by His precious blood made us new creatures in Him!

Therefore if any man be *in Christ, he is a new creature:* old things are passed away; behold, all things are become new. (2 Corinthians 5:17, emphasis added)

I became aware that now that I had been washed with the blood of the Lord Jesus Christ. He had a claim over me, and I was His: *"...but now in Christ Jesus ye who sometimes were far off are made nigh [near] by the blood of Christ"* (Ephesians 2:13). *His daughter, the daughter of a King!* I was beautiful inside, cleansed whiter than snow.

The king's daughter is all glorious within: her clothing is of wrought gold. (Psalm 45:13, emphasis added)

I had a heritage and a claim to Heaven—His throne and my home, *the King's palace*—and I would one day enter it with gladness and rejoicing.

With gladness and rejoicing shall they be brought: they shall enter into *the king's palace.* (Psalm 45:15, emphasis added)

I had done nothing to deserve salvation, but I thank the Lord Jesus for His free gift of salvation to an undeserving sinner such as me. It was His mercy and grace and an abundance of kindness and love that made Him reach down to unworthy people such as me!

...the holy scriptures, which are able to make thee wise unto salvation through *faith which is in Christ Jesus.* (2 Timothy 3:15, emphasis added)

Chapter 32

INVITING SANDRA

...he that hath my word, let him speak
my word faithfully. (Jeremiah 23:28)

Excited to share the transformation in my life I had experienced from reading the New Testament, I felt an urgency to invite my school friend, Sandra, to our home. A weekday would be best because no one else would be home, I surmised. I told my parents that a school friend would be coming over. To my surprise, they accepted the idea without any disagreement!

After sharing a light lunch, I couldn't wait to highlight the value of the treasure she had given me. I started by telling Sandra that I had acknowledged that I was a sinner and accepted the Lord Jesus Christ as my personal Saviour. I continued by telling her how I was now a *changed person* from reading the Bible!

Uncomfortable silence filled the room after I finished my enthusiastic talk! Sandra's puzzled expression as she studied me betrayed her disinterest in the subject. Although she remained speechless and emotionless, it was *obvious* she did not feel my passion nor value the profound and precious message that I had just shared with her.

She became restless, wanting to leave. I tried to prolong her stay by inviting her to my bedroom.

Disappointed that I could not continue my story, I led her to my room. Trying to keep her interested enough to stay, I showed her my collection of brooches. They instantly captured her curiosity, especially the hand-carved ivory one my cousin had brought for me from India. My mother worked for a factory where they cut old clothes, and often she would find brooches pinned to scraps of cloth. She would bring home these unique brooches, and I would ask her if I could keep them, as they fascinated me. She allowed me to collect them in a box after I had carefully cleaned and polished them. I prized my collection of about seventy of varying colours, sizes, and designs.

I told Sandra that my mother had given them to me. As I watched her examine each one inquisitively, she stated she was invited to a party and needed *a* brooch for her outfit, wanting to borrow just *one*. I told her she was welcome to borrow one. As she spent more time going over the unique pieces of metal art, she alleged she was not sure which one would best complement her outfit. After some time, she selected fifteen to twenty, including my ivory brooch. She assured me repeatedly she would take good care of them and return them soon after the event. I felt uneasy about whether she was telling the truth about her party, or conveniently using this excuse to steal from me. Nevertheless, I let her take part of my collection.

A few weeks after her supposed event, I called Sandra to ask her to return my brooches. At first, she told me that she was going away. After a few more conversations, she informed me that all the brooches were lost. In the last conversation, she wanted to meet up with me to purchase a necklace to replace all the lost brooches. We met at a department store where she selected an inexpensive plain wooden necklace, paid for it, handed it to me, and then said goodbye. It saddened me to think that she had stolen from me, and never had the intention of returning my belongings. It was hard to lose some of the best brooches in my collection, but being betrayed by someone I had thought I could trust was *worse*.

I still had Sandra's phone number, and found out that she was going to the same university as I was, but in the engineering program. I called her several times, leaving messages with her dad. She never returned my calls. On the last phone call, her father scolded me for calling and told me she was at a bar drinking with her friends. He added that Sandra never wanted to hear from me again. I held my breath as he hung up. I felt betrayed.

A few days later, my mother came into my room asking for the brooches. She took them to my dad, who inspected each one. What followed was a conversation indicating my dad was going to take them to work to *show* the ladies in his office. They assured me they would be returned to me. Despite my refusal, he took them on his nightshift. After repeatedly asking him to return them, I somehow found out that the women had admired them and distributed all of them amongst themselves! I felt cheated and tricked once again, but wondered if the office workers knew they were taken from me—and then realized they were *never* mine to begin with.

Unfortunately, I was heartbroken that Sandra valued the brooches more than she did my testimony about how her gift, the Gideon New Testament, had changed my life forever. It seemed that she rejected the Truth of the Gospel, but I hoped it would be only temporary and that she would realize the worth of the message I had shared with her every time she looked at my brooches.

What are a few brooches in comparison to the free gift of salvation offered to us at no cost? How much more should we reach out to others with the same generosity that God has shown towards us!

For we preach… Christ Jesus the Lord… (2 Corinthians 4:5)

…we preach Christ crucified… Christ the power of God, and the wisdom of God. (1 Corinthians 1:23–24)

Chapter 33

New Life in Christ Jesus

And ye shall know the *truth*, and the
truth shall make you *free*… If the Son
therefore shall make you *free*,
ye shall be *free* indeed.
(John 8:32, 36, emphasis added)

…the *truth* is in Jesus…
(Ephesians 4:21, emphasis added)

In my early years, I had many questions about life and our existence. Not only were many of these vital questions finally answered, but they were answered by a God Who worked behind the scenes to one day reveal His plan for my life. He made a ragged, worthless woman into a new creature.

> That they may see, and know, and consider, and understand together, that the hand of the LORD hath done this…
> (Isaiah 41:20)

I extend my utmost gratitude, adoration, and praise to the Almighty God, the Father, for choosing me to see beauty in the Lord Jesus Christ, through the powerful work of the Holy

Spirit, using His precious Word, the Bible, to minister to me. In His master plan, according to His wisdom, He orchestrated and ordered all the circumstances in my life, so systematically and skillfully, to achieve His eternal purpose by giving me true freedom through the Truth in Jesus Christ!

It has been a thrill and a privilege to share my life story about what the Lord Jesus Christ, the Creator of the Universe, has marvelously done for me. No doubt there is much missing in this book about how His grace worked in my life, which will be more fully and completely revealed in Heaven!

It has been remarkable how God's work in my life in the spiritual realm worked in parallel to my emotional and physical journey. Though I was unaware of what He was doing, He brought to fruition His will.

I chose to give the reader a feeling of my complex journey: the emotions, the struggles, the helplessness, and finally the resolution and outcome. Many of the answers I discovered can be applied to anything you may be going through. Life could have a deeper meaning for you on this earth—and ultimately in Heaven with the Lord Jesus Christ.

What is beyond astounding is that amidst a very strict home life, being isolated from society, the Lord ingeniously introduced me to Christianity through various means despite my circumstances. Although a children's Bible storybook and yearly Gideon New Testaments were thrown out, God used other means to reach out to me. On a few occasions, singing hymns in school gave me a sense of His presence. When a classmate brought in a Bible storybook to school, I asked her to bring it back so I could copy one of its pages for a contest with *love* as its theme. Seeing the picture of a Person called Jesus preaching love to people stirred my heart.

Two momentous events occurred with the Lord's direct intervention. Firstly, I found a booklet of Bible verses on the ground in a laneway shortly after a night of desperately crying to an unknown God, having made up my mind to commit suicide. The Lord Jesus drew near and met me there to provide me the most precious gift, His Word. He was aware of my sadness and my need in my lonely walk.

…Jesus himself drew near, and went with them… And he said unto them, What manner of communications are these that ye have… as ye walk, and are sad? (Luke 24:15, 17)

Secondly, I met a classmate at a street intersection from whom I was able to get a Gideon New Testament, although she turned out to be an atheist. God's power commanded the light of the gospel of Jesus Christ to shine out of the darkness to give me understanding through His Word:

For God, who commanded *the light* to shine out of darkness, hath shined in our hearts, to give *the light of the knowledge of the glory of God in the face of Jesus Christ.* (2 Corinthians 4:6, emphasis added)

Both situations were perfectly planned with precision by a wise and a faithful God. The four months I was home alone from school were incredibly prepared by God to allow me to focus and read the Bible, which led me to the amazing Lord Jesus Christ when I was hungering for the Truth.

I did not consciously know the statement *"I AM THAT I AM"* found in Exodus 3:14. This was the name God gave to Moses to identify Himself to the children of Israel. I had seen an iconic movie, the Ten Commandments, and the Spirit of God brought the subconsciously stored phrase in my memory to my remembrance at the proper time when I was questioned by my friend at her home. This wonderful name of God in the Old Testament is the "I AM" of the New Testament, the Lord Jesus Christ: *"Verily, verily, I say unto you, Before Abraham was, I am"* (John 8:58, emphasis added).

The Lord Jesus made many references to Himself as the I AM in the New Testament. The Lord said *I Am* the Way, the Truth, the Life, the Door, the Bread of Life, the Good Shepherd, the Light, and the Resurrection.

While telling my story has made it necessary to disclose and acknowledge my background, it has not been my intention to dishonour, blame, or provoke animosity towards my family members. Rather, I wish to highlight how God used unpleasant and difficult situations to accomplish His purposes. When I was forsaken, the Lord Jesus in His faithfulness took me up to protect and shield me from making bad decisions, to heal my traumatized life and steer me for His ultimate purpose, to bring beauty out of the ashes and make the valley of death into a well, ultimately bringing glory to His Name and offering me a beautiful end, one of promise and hope for a better future and a new relationship with a known God.

> ...to appoint unto them that mourn... to give unto them beauty for ashes, the oil of joy for mourning, the garment of praise for the spirit of heaviness... the LORD, that he might be glorified. (Isaiah 61:3)

> Who passing through the valley of Baca [death] make it a well... (Psalm 84:6)

Even my childhood illnesses were a feature controlled by the Almighty God in His wise plan to skillfully work in my life so every incident, every heartache, every pain had a part in the orchestration of a bigger plan.

Though my parents lacked medical knowledge and education, were not aware of the seriousness of my health issues, and didn't provide the attention that would have led to medical care and treatment, the Lord saw to it that this trial would only go as far as He would allow it. He was working to bring me down to the depths of despair. I would only be willing to listen and hear His voice once my heart was *plowed enough* to receive His Word!

As I look back at my childhood, I know the Lord knew all along the crisis I was in. He systematically worked each event with His perfect wisdom to accomplish His purposes. Whatever cross we are asked to bear, may we do it thankfully, without animosity or bitterness, realizing our God is in control and does all things well.

The circumstances of my health do not leave me with bitterness toward anyone mentioned, but a heartfelt prayer for these I loved and will always love; through their own suffering and cultural upbringing, they had to conform to the customs, pressures, and biases of the day.

In those early years, my interactions with family were less than desirable. Even though my life may have seemed like a *curse*, the Lord God was in absolute control of how far He would allow people, His valuable tools, to affect me and to bring me to the end of myself. Although I experienced hardship, neglect, and prejudice, I admit that social and personal pressures, religious and cultural norms, financial limitations, and superstitions contributed to their behaviour. In their busy life, their ignorance of my condition and lack of medical knowledge precipitated my abandonment. When I was in desperate need, He opened my eyes, and made me willing to hear His still small voice, balm to my broken heart. He created a longing within me so deep, no human resource would be enough to rescue me. He eventually opened my heart and eyes to see the altogether lovely One, Jesus Christ!

> ... the LORD thy God turned the curse into *a blessing unto thee,* because *the LORD thy God loved thee.* (Deuteronomy 23:5, emphasis added)

Both my grandmother and my mother were instruments used by God to create a deep-rooted need and a yearning heart for the Truth, at last leading me to the Lord Jesus Christ.

My grandmother's tender and loving care was my first introduction to *love*. Her absence from my life in Canada amplified the loneliness I felt. Nightly, I wet my pillow with tears as I remembered my happy memories with her and craved her presence.

My mother's cultural views, personal biases, and past turmoil triggered her abandonment of care and love for me. I longed to have a connection with her. I wanted her to acknowledge my existence. Instead of being her daughter, I was an unwanted object and a nuisance interfering with her daily life.

Both women were equally significant as *tools* in God's hands to draw me to the end of myself and force me to surrender my own will. Only then could I accept the grace and mercy freely available to me in the arms of the Lord Jesus Christ.

As I bring both my grandmother and my mother to the throne of God, my prayer has been for them to experience the same grace, mercy, and blessing I tasted, that they will enjoy the freedom of knowing their Creator, the True and Living God, and that they will turn away from the stronghold and blindness of Hinduism.

The treatment received by the Lord Jesus at the hands of wicked men was evil; nonetheless, He interceded and forgave these ignorant and blind people who tortured and crucified Him on the cross. He exhorts us to exhibit forgiveness and love to those who have hurt us—whether intentionally or ignorantly. As He said, *"Father, forgive them; for they know not what they do"* (Luke 23:34).

The Lord Jesus Christ has given those of us who believe in Him the capacity and willingness to forgive the people who have harmed us, and even to love them. In my case, I thank God that these experiences led me to meeting Jesus, and I forgive my family!

As you have read this book, may you appreciate it as a love story about the Saviour—the Lord Jesus Christ—and His search and love for the sinner. This love is divine, unfathomable, and incomprehensible! This story is about One Who came to *"seek and to save that which was lost"* (Luke 19:10). I was lost in the spiritual darkness of Hinduism for eighteen years.

Scripture makes it clear that idolatry is sinful and blasphemous to the True and Living God. These idols are powerless in redeeming a soul for heaven. They are incapable of offering peace and love or deliverance to a hurting person.

> ...the heathen... Their idols are silver and gold, the work of men's hands. They have mouths, but they speak not: eyes have they, but they see not: They have ears, but they hear not: noses have they, but they smell not: They have hands, but they handle not: feet have they, but they walk not: neither speak they through their throat. (Psalm 115:2–7)

The True and Living God's work of salvation in my life allowed me to turn from the idols and to serve Him:

...how ye turned to God from idols *to serve the living and true God;* and to wait for his Son from heaven, whom he raised from the dead, even Jesus, which delivered us from the wrath to come. (1 Thessalonians 1:9–10, emphasis added)

Even though I did not even know He existed, the Lord watched over me from Heaven on high, touched by my loneliness, pain, and sorrow. He waited for the perfect time to miraculously deliver me from physical and spiritual death by drawing me with His everlasting love to faith in Christ Jesus. Finding me brought joy to God's heart and a rejoicing in Heaven!

...Yea, I have loved thee with an *everlasting love:* therefore with *loving kindness* have I drawn thee. (Jeremiah 31:3, emphasis added)

When I was without strength, by *grace* He reached down to my lowly, helpless state, bought me with His precious blood, made me into a new creature in Him, and endowed me with the gift of eternal life and a forever promise to be with Him in His Home in Heaven.

For when we were *without strength,* in due time Christ died for the ungodly. (Romans 5:6, emphasis added)

The way the Holy Spirit used the power of the Scriptures to minister to my heart was profound, life-changing, and truly outstanding. If you are searching to solve the mystery of life, God provides all the answers to your questions in His complete book, the Bible, and will give you understanding through His Spirit, our Comforter, with your eyes opened to the Truth of God. Not only did the Scriptures prove to be precious, instructive, and comforting, but they exposed God's language of love to a destitute sinner—me. God's Word promises to accomplish what He sent it out to do, and not return void:

> ...so shall *my word* be that goeth forth out of my mouth: it shall not return unto me void, but it shall *accomplish* that which I please, and it shall *prosper* in the thing whereto I sent it. (Isaiah 55:11, emphasis added)

Just as a potter takes a formless piece of clay to shape the vessel for his own choosing, the Almighty God permitted these occurrences to *touch* me, *break* me, and *re-mould* me, ultimately creating a vessel for His use and for my eternal blessing.

> But now, O LORD, thou art our father; we are the clay, and thou our potter; and we all are *the work of thy hand.* (Isaiah 64:8, emphasis added)

God granted me His approval and gave me a new hope, a new purpose, and a new eternal destiny to fulfill all that I was searching for. His work in me—somebody who seemed to be a pitiful and worthless person in society—was to create a new creature in the image of His beloved Son, a future King. He gave me a new relationship with Him.

> Therefore if any man be in Christ, he is a *new creature*: old things are passed away; behold, all things are become new. (2 Corinthians 5:17, emphasis added)

In the world's estimation, I was worthless, weak, and unimportant, but despite its evaluation of me, God choose me to make me worthy for His use. May the glory be His!

...not many wise... not many mighty, not many noble, are called: But God hath *chosen* the foolish things of the world to confound the wise; and God hath *chosen* the weak things of the world to confound the things which are mighty; And base things of the world, and things which are despised, hath God *chosen*... (1 Corinthians 1:26–28, emphasis added)

The Lord Jesus Christ gave me worth as a pearl of great price, dignity as a woman with a purpose, and meaning and a reason to live. I am a witness to His transformative power to turn an impossible situation into blessings for His glory!

The Lord God chose me because He loved me!

...the LORD thy God hath *chosen* thee... because the LORD loved you... the LORD brought you out with a mighty hand, and *redeemed* you out of the house of bondmen... (Deuteronomy 7:6, 8)

I have not written this book because I am better than anyone else, or greatly skilled in writing, or endowed with any skills or special gifts. But I am also not worse than anyone else because I am a woman... because I am brown... or because I am a Christian. It is truly extraordinary that I was chosen before the foundation of the earth, given faith to believe in the one and only way of salvation, washed in the precious blood of the Lamb, and accepted by the Almighty God. As a redeemed child of God, a child of the King, I can humbly and gratefully declare myself as His daughter—the *King's Daughter!* Praise be to Him!

As Ruth in the Old Testament asked: *"Why have I found <u>grace</u> in thine eyes, that thou shouldest take knowledge of me, seeing I am a stranger?"* (2:10, emphasis added).

Why did the Lord Jesus bestow such grace upon me? Because He is the One Who is *"full of grace and truth"* (John 1:14). He reached out with His everlasting divine love, delighting to have communion with me, and allowing me to become part of His family. I praise Him as my marvelous and awesome God. As I wrote in a poem years ago,

> Oh, that the world doesn't see the beauty,
> O Lord in Thee!
> Oh, how the world doesn't know:
> how the heart can be satisfied in Thee!
> How is it that Thou hast shown this to me,
> seeing I am but a stranger?

The yearning to see my family come to the Lord Jesus Christ has given me the God-given urgency to use every opportunity to reach out to others with the Gospel. This is either by distribution of Bibles, calendars, or tracts conveying the Truth about Jesus Christ, or by speaking to those the Lord brings my way.

> But as for you, ye thought evil against me; but *God meant it unto good,* to bring to pass, as it is this day, to save much people alive. (Genesis 50:20, emphasis added)

> But I would ye should understand, brethren, that the things which happened unto me have fallen out rather unto *the furtherance of the gospel...* (Philippians 1:12, emphasis added)

Jesus Christ, both God and Man, was sent for the unbelievers, the lost, the bound, the prisoners, the hurt and destitute, to deliver them and offer them salvation. He is the only One to reconcile us to God by His sacrifice on the cross for our sins two thousand years ago—the only way to Heaven. He is risen and is presently sitting on the right hand of the Majesty on High!

No matter what crisis you may be facing in your unique journey, be assured that the Lord Jesus Christ is interested in your emotional, physical, mental, and spiritual welfare. His tender care and immense love amid your trial can satisfy and heal you emotionally and mentally. Your heart, made by Him, can only be filled with Him—nothing else will ever gratify but *Jesus Christ Himself.* He can use circumstances for your benefit, performing miracles in your life. God reveals His heart of forgiveness by offering you salvation—a relationship with His Beloved Son, the Lord Jesus Christ—which will preserve you for life everlasting by making you suitable to stand in His presence. May the work of the Lord Jesus Christ displayed in my life attract you to His beauty and majesty!

My prayer is that God would use this book to bless, fortify, encourage, inspire, and strengthen you, and give hope and solace in your journey. He cares about whatever you may be going through, and delights to demonstrate His amazing eternal, unconditional, and immeasurable love. Yield to Him today and watch what wonders He can do for you, too! I dearly hope that your heart will be open to His message and your eyes will see Jesus Christ in all His brilliance. May you rest in His power and watch Him change your life.

There is one key verse in the *Little Bible* booklet I found that had a deep meaning for me, and I have recited it frequently, wanting it to be the motto of my life: *"And call upon me in the day of trouble: I will deliver thee, and thou shalt glorify me"* (Psalm 50:15).

When I was in the *day of trouble* with depression and loneliness, the Lord Jesus delivered me. In accordance with this verse, it has been my honour and desire to *glorify Him* by sharing what He has done for me. He gave me His Word, and I trust I spoke it faithfully to display His magnificent attributes so you would be attracted to the beauty of this Incredible Person, your Creator, the Son of God: *"…he that hath my word, let him speak my word faithfully"* (Jeremiah 23:28).

> The law of the Lord is perfect, converting the soul: the testimony of the Lord is sure, making wise the simple.
>
> The statutes of the Lord are right, rejoicing the heart: the commandment of the Lord is pure, enlightening the eyes.
>
> The fear of the Lord is clean, enduring for ever: the judgments of the Lord are true and righteous altogether.
>
> More to be desired are they than gold, yea, than much fine gold: sweeter also than honey and the honeycomb. (Psalm 19:7–10)

Who is this King of glory? The LORD of hosts, he is the King of glory. (Psalm 24:10)

...he is Lord of lords, and King of kings: and they that are with him are called, and chosen, and faithful. (Revelation 17:14)

...O most mighty, with thy glory and thy majesty... Thy throne, O God, is for ever and ever: the sceptre of thy kingdom is a right sceptre. Thou lovest righteousness, and hatest wickedness... Kings' daughters were among thy honourable women... Hearken, O daughter, and consider, and incline thine ear: forget also thine own people, and thy father's house; so shall the king greatly desire thy beauty: for he is thy Lord; and worship thou him... The king's daughter is all glorious within: her clothing is of wrought gold. She shall be brought unto the king... With gladness and rejoicing shall they be brought: they shall enter into the king's palace... therefore shall the people praise thee for ever and ever. (Psalm 45:3–17)

For God so loved the world, that he gave his only begotten Son, that whosoever believeth in him should not perish, but have everlasting life. (John 3:16)

About the Author

Rajkumari Moksha, brought up in a strict Hindu household for twenty-six years, feels compelled to share her story about meeting the Lord Jesus Christ, Who changed her life.

She has been a Christian for over forty-six years, involved in children's ministry and the worldwide distribution of the gospel. She has also been active as a speaker and a healthcare professional for a number of years, and an entrepreneur of her own healthcare business for fourteen years.

Married for over thirty-seven years, she and her loving and supportive husband have raised three incredible children, with a growing family.

Rajkumari's deepest passion has been to share her faith in Jesus Christ to all those whom she meets in her travels and in the community.

The King's Daughter, short-listed by Word Alive Press, is her first book. The sequel, *Accepted in the Beloved*, will further detail her life as a Christian within the Hindu community.